Perfect Phrases for Perfect Hiring

Also available from McGraw-Hill

Perfect Phrases for Executive Presentations by
Alan M. Perlman

Perfect Phrases for Performance Reviews by
Douglas Max and Robert Bacal

Perfect Solutions for Difficult Employee Situations by
Sid Kemp

Perfect Phrases for Customer Service by
Robert Bacal

Perfect Phrases for Business Proposals and Business Plans by
Don Debelak

Perfect Phrases for the Sales Call by
William T. Brooks

Perfect Phrases for Perfect Hiring

Hundreds of Ready-to-Use Phrases for Interviewing and Hiring the Best Employees

Lori Davila and Margot King

McGraw-Hill

New York   Chicago   San Francisco   Lisbon
London   Madrid   Mexico City   Milan   New Delhi
San Juan   Seoul   Singapore   Sydney   Toronto

1 2 3 4 5 6 7 8 9 0   FGR/FGR   0 9 8 7

ISBN-13: 978-0-07-148170-0
ISBN-10:   0-07-148170-2

McGraw-Hill books are available at special discounts to use as premiums and sales promotions, or for use in corporate training programs. For more information, please write to the Director of Special Sales, McGraw-Hill, Two Penn Plaza, New York, NY 10121-2298. Or contact your local bookstore.

Dedication

To my husband, who gives me continual life support; my daughter, who is my source of pride; and lastly, my beloved mother, who has always been my inspiration.

Margot King

To my mother, my beloved father, and to my husband for their devotion as parents, spouses, and children.

Lori Davila

Contents

Foreword   ix
Introduction   xi

Part One. Developing a Hiring Game Plan   1

1. Define Your Ideal Candidates   3
Define the Right Job Profile 5
Get a Group Consensus on the Right Profile 12
Phrases for Writing Job Descriptions 16
Conclusion 33

2. Find and Attract the Right Talent   35
Target the Right Candidate 35
Write Compelling Advertising Copy 36
Data Mining 41
Target Professional Associations 43

3. How to Choose a Third-Party Recruiter   53
When Do You Use a Third-Party Recruiter? 53
Evaluate Service Options 54

Part Two. Screening, Interviewing, and Evaluating Candidates   75

4. Prescreening Candidates   77
*There are tremendous benefits to prescreening
your candidate pool: 77*

Contents

5. Conduct a Productive Interview 93
Set Up an Interview 93
An interview is divided up into three parts: 98

6. Conduct Due Diligence of Final Candidates 127

7. Manage Candidates and Their Interest Effectively 145

Part Three. Hiring and Transitioning Top People into Your Organization 159

8. Negotiate an Offer Without Any Hitches 161
Is It All About the Money? 161
Counter the Counteroffer 171

9. Make Your New Employees Feel at Home 173

Foreword

A s I waited on line the other day at my local coffee shop, a feeling came over me that I realized I have had many times before. The server behind the counter was desperately struggling to keep up with the pace of the early morning coffee rush. Unable (or unwilling) to stay focused on the task at hand and juggle multiple customers requests simultaneously, each order took what seemed like an eternity to fill. After observing the server for a while (I was in line for 15 minutes!), it wasn't hard to see that this person was a poor match for his job. As I left with my coffee (containing sugar that I hadn't ordered), I thought to myself, "Who hired this guy . . . and more importantly *why*?

I don't know about you, but unfortunately for me situations like this one are all too common. It's possible that I notice them more because I've spent 20 years as a Recruiter, HR Generalist, and hiring manager. Nevertheless, if you're like me, you can't help wondering, "If people are an organization's most important asset, why can't they do a better job picking the right people? Don't they see how damaging the wrong people can be to their business?"

For the last decade, I've been working with a wide range of organizations as a Consultant for Novations, Inc., a global HR consulting and training firm. Through this work, I've discovered that there are a whole host of answers to this question. For many organizations, they don't even know that they have a problem. For others, they see the problem as unavoidable, a necessary cost of doing business. After all, hiring isn't a *science*, is it? Perhaps not, but there certainly are things that can be done to maximize the likelihood of getting the right person in the right job.

But where does that leave you? If you're fortunate enough to be part of an organization that already has a structured selection process and tools in place, you've got a head start. Regardless of your starting point, however, this book will provide you with the information you need to begin doing your part. Lori and Margot masterfully describe the entire selection process, from developing a hiring game plan all the way through to on-boarding the new hire successfully.

As a recruiter and hiring manager, even after I learned all the right steps in the process and had all the right tools, I struggled with what to say and how. For those of you like me, this book will be truly a gift. At each step in the process, the authors suggest words for you to use ("perfect phrases") in order to maximize your impact. Whether you use the phrases exactly as written or you put them into your own words, by the time you put down this book you will be infinitely more prepared to hire right each and every time. After all, none of us want to be the one who causes a customer to ask the question "Who hired that guy, and *why*?" do we?

Tim Vigue
Executive Consultant—Selection, Novations Group, Inc.
www.novations.com

Introduction

I f you've picked up this book, it's probably because you're looking for help with your hiring efforts. If so, you are acutely aware that the most important responsibility you have is to select the right employees who will best contribute to your company's mission.

Maybe you've hired people into your organization that looked perfect from the outside but disappointed you once they joined your team, leaving you baffled by your lack of ability to identify the red flags upfront. Perhaps your organization has a reputation for being a "revolving door" of employees coming and going and you don't know how to change that pattern. Maybe you've had a hiring success story and you're unsure of how to replicate it. Or perhaps you are expanding your organization and you are faced with an overwhelming search for candidates, and you desperately want to get it right the first time.

Whatever your particular situation, your feelings of dissatisfaction when it comes to hiring may stem from the advice you've been given from your colleagues and hiring experts. You've more than likely been told that to be successful, you must have a schematic in place and that by simply planning in advance, you will achieve a high level of success. After all, hiring superstars does not occur by accident. But if this is the case then why, after all the preparation, didn't your last hire work out?

Introduction

Careful planning along with the flawless execution of a well-structured hiring process is just part of the hiring puzzle. Constructing a communications strategy—what impressions you want to convey by what you say and what messages you want to emphasize by the phrases you choose—is equally critical to attracting and retaining the right employees for your organization. Your chosen words will determine the kinds of relationships you develop and the trust that you build with candidates, references, and new hires. Likewise, the quality of information you are able to extract from them will determine the future success of your newly hired employees.

At every step, from sourcing to recruiting to reference checking to employee orientation and all the way through to onboarding, you will need to intentionally clarify what impression you want to leave. That is why it is so important to prepare phrases and questions to help you attract the right candidates, obtain data to make the right decisions regarding the candidate and cultural fit, and to ensure the early-stage success of your new employees.

How you communicate with candidates throughout the hiring process can determine whether or not they stick around and remain excited about your opportunity. For example, clearly prepared phrases can improve relationships so that you get better answers to your questions from candidates and references. And, if you create an environment conducive to openness, the result will be improved performance and productivity once a new employee is on board, and problems that may arise will be solved more efficiently.

This book provides you with the sample phrases and questions you need to prepare a communications strategy that will attract the best candidates, grab their attention, and hold on to them. You will find sample phrases to help you identify your ideal candidates, attract appropriate talent, effectively choose third party recruiting help, prescreen candidates, conduct successful interviews, perform due diligence of your final candidates, manage candidate interest, make job offers, and get your new employees off on the right foot, resulting in improved productivity, retention, and motivation of your new employees.

This book will give you the ammunition to maximize the impact of every word and syllable you speak during the hiring process. To underestimate the importance of preparing your statements is to potentially short circuit your entire hiring effort: In order to attract what you want, your words will need to be works of art, compelling to the extreme. Fortunately, your statements can be prepared and practiced before each phase of your game plan, from screening and interviewing to evaluating, hiring, and onboarding.

The phrases you are about to read will allow you to avoid legal mishaps; identify and excite the right fit candidates; obtain good quality references that open up; get insightful answers to interview questions so you can properly evaluate candidates; prescreen efficiently so you're not wasting time interviewing the wrong candidates; avoid mishaps when making offers and before candidates start work; and improve productivity, motivation, and worth once new employees are on board.

Perfect Phrases for Perfect Hiring will help you avoid surprises by using the right phrases while maintaining a personal and open approach every step of the way.

Part One

Developing a Hiring Game Plan

Chapter 1

Define Your Ideal Candidates

The most important step in hiring the perfect employee is also the very first step—clearly defining what you need (not just what you want) in a candidate so that your overall organization, not just you, will significantly benefit from your hiring decision. To find your "match made in heaven," start by identifying key factors that describe the *whole person* you are looking for. Look for skills and qualities that have been learned, that can be learned, and that can't be learned, but also be aware of some other important aspects such as the candidate's motivation and drive. For example, if someone has learned a software program or two, having to learn another program may be less important than hiring a person who is genuinely motivated and possesses a passion for helping others resolve issues in a customer service role. Ranking a candidate's performance and personal skills/qualities higher than a technical skill that can be learned on the job is something to consider.

Start your needs assessment by identifying these key areas for your open position:

- **Technical Knowledge and Skills.** These are learned skills obtained through education and/or on-the-job training. Examples include software programs, accounting expertise, and effective advertising strategies.

- **Performance Skills.** These are required skills that go above and beyond the technical skills and are usually part of a person's inherent makeup. Examples of these skills include planning and organizing, customer service orientation, relationship building, analyzing, and strategic thinking.
- **Personal Qualities and Motivations.** These are also ingrained in a person's makeup and are nearly impossible to obtain satisfactorily as a learned behavior. These qualities will reveal if a candidate *will* do the job, not just if he *can* do the job. Examples include initiative, adaptability, competitiveness, and goal orientation.
- **Other Qualifications.** Minimum requirements to do the job, such as educational degree and years of experience in a particular field.

Unfortunately, the majority of hiring managers spend little to no time defining candidate qualifications because their primary work responsibilities have a way of piling up and demanding all of their attentions. Ironically, a lack of focus on this crucial step is often the leading cause of business pain, loss, disruption, and extraordinary expenses. Don't get caught in this trap! Keep the following points in mind:

- It's impossible to properly recruit, screen, and evaluate candidates without knowing the specifics of what you are looking for.
- Your success in hiring employees who will add value and flourish within your organization is directly related to how well you perform this initial step of defining requirements in the hiring process.
- It is advisable to tackle this step with other key stakeholders in your organization so that down the road,

those who have an interest in the open position can't change their minds or influence a hiring decision that is not in the best interest of the company. You can conduct a facilitated brainstorming session where key decision makers can participate in, guide, and approve the job definition process, or you can circulate a job description template to your team along with questions. Request that questionnaires come back to a central point for compilation, editing, and then reissue for final approval.

■ To clarify qualifications, seek out others who are currently holding or have previously held the open position. Also consider getting feedback from team members, peers, and managers of the position, as well as other external and internal contacts who will regularly interact with the position, such as Human Resources and other key influencers. You may not be able to see all of the needs of the open position yourself, so working with others who have different perspectives will ensure that checks and balances are in place.

■ Avoid the number one hiring mistake—hiring someone in your mirror image. It is human nature to gravitate to people we like—people with common interests, values, and personalities; however, when we do this, we're putting the true needs of the organization last.

Define the Right Job Profile

Defining the right profile for your open position requires the creation of a detailed job description containing the following specific items:

- **Position Title**
- **Relationships and Roles**—description of whom this employee reports to, who reports to this employee, and other working relationships.
- **Job Specifics**—name of the division or department, geographic location, salary grade/range, employee status (full-time, part-time, contractor, etc.), travel requirements, and start date.
- **Position Purpose**—summary describing the nature, level, purpose, and objective of the job (usually three sentences or fewer).
- **Duties and Responsibilities**—list of duties, essential functions, continuing responsibilities, and accountabilities of the position. Each responsibility that comprises of at least 5 percent of the employee's time should be included. Determine the percentage of these duties in relation to the total job and note them accordingly.
- **Job Qualifications**—the minimum qualifications, specifications, and standards required to perform the essential functions of the job. Tie qualifications directly to the job duties and include areas such as education, licenses, certifications, experience, knowledge, and skills.
- **Other Physical, Environmental, Mental, and Special Requirements**—list other demands that are required for performing the essential functions. Examples include climbing ladders, standing for long periods of time, lifting materials up to 50 pounds, reading documents or instruments, reasoning, utilizing computers in a PC Windows environment, and heavy travel schedules.

A well-developed job description provides insurmountable benefits. It ensures that everyone involved in hiring the new employee is on the same page during all recruiting, screening, interviewing, and decision-making efforts. It also provides the new hire with an understanding of the accountabilities, duties, and responsibilities she is expected to fulfill, alleviating future misunderstandings and conflicts. See the Sample Job Description Template, next page.

Sample Job Description Template

Job Title: Sales Training Manager
Reports To: Director of Sales
Supervises: Field Sales Trainers and Curriculum Designers
Department: Sales
Location: Decatur, Georgia
Salary Grade: 12
Employee Status: Regular full-time
Travel: 50 percent overnight travel
Date: Month/Date/Year

Position Purpose: Develop, manage, and execute all sales training programs to include initial new hire sales training and continued advanced sales training.

Duties and Responsibilities:

1. Develop, manage, and execute all sales training programs under the direction of Director of Sales (50 percent).
2. Work with Director of Medical Education and Product Training Manager to incorporate clinical learning and best adult learning processes into sales training programs (5 percent).
3. Coach Territory Managers to maintain a high level of proficiency with selling skills and product knowledge through direct rides with Territory Managers and by developing improvement plans with Regional Managers (10 percent).
4. Coordinate field rides and competency checks with Field Sales Trainers (5 percent).

5. Conduct selling skill assessments in the field by working with Territory Managers identified by the Regional Manager and Director of Sales (10 percent).
6. Ensure corporate image is maintained and marketed professionally (5 percent).
7. Participate in scheduled sales management meetings and trade show events (5 percent).
8. Develop sales training programs during major trade shows and events as required (10 percent).

Qualifications: Must be a leader and be able to perform each essential duty satisfactorily. The requirements listed below are representative of the knowledge, skills, and/or abilities required. Reasonable accommodations may be made to enable individuals with disabilities to perform the essential functions.

- Strong initiative and leadership skills.
- Demonstrated patience with teaching/coaching situations.
- Excellent communication skills, both verbal and written.
- Strong analytical and problem-solving abilities.
- Able to adapt quickly and react positively to business needs and changes in strategies.
- Excellent interpersonal skills and ability to work successfully with a variety of people.
- Willingness to set and maintain high standards of performance.

Education/Experience: Bachelor's degree (BA) from a four-year college or university; a minimum four years related experience and/or training; or equivalent combination of

➡

education and experience as deemed appropriate by the Director of Sales. Either have or be willing to study adult learning processes to effectively develop training programs.

Language Ability: In English, must have ability to read, analyze, and interpret general business periodicals, professional journals, technical procedures, or governmental regulations. Possess the ability to write reports, business correspondence, and procedure manuals, as well as effectively present information and respond to questions from groups of managers, clients, customers, and the general public. Must be comfortable speaking to large groups of people and have a demonstrated ability to teach both individuals and groups.

Math Ability: Ability to calculate figures and amounts, such as discounts, interest, commissions, proportions, percentages, area, circumference, and volume.

Reasoning Ability: Ability to solve practical problems and deal with a variety of concrete variables in situations where only limited standardization exists. Ability to interpret a variety of instructions furnished in written, oral, diagram, or schedule form.

Computer Skills: Microsoft: Word, Excel, PowerPoint, Access, Outlook, Internet software, order processing, database software, contact management.

Work Environment: The work environment characteristics described here are representative of those an employee encounters while performing the essential functions of this job. Reasonable accommodations may be made to enable individuals with disabilities to perform the essential functions.

While performing the duties of this job, the employee is regularly exposed to outside weather conditions, and it is at his sole discretion on how adverse weather should be managed as it relates to the needs of the position.

Expected overnight travel requirement will be up to 50 percent, depending upon the time of year and strategic needs of the company.

Physical Demands: The physical demands described here are representative of those that must be met by an employee to successfully perform the essential functions of this job. Reasonable accommodations may be made to enable individuals with disabilities to perform the essential functions.

The employee is occasionally required to lift up to 50 pounds.

Get a Group Consensus on the Right Profile

The following is a sampling of questions you can share with those who know the position best. The answers received will help you create the best job description in terms of responsibilities and cultural fit.

Relationships and Roles

- Working relationships are the continuing contacts with whom the incumbent must interface to accomplish the duties of the position. List the major interactions the position has with others inside and outside the organization (clients, vendors, partners, press contacts, etc.) and briefly describe the purpose or result of these contacts.
- Does the position have supervisory responsibilities, internally or externally? If so, list the number and titles of the employees that report to this position.

Position Purpose

- What is the purpose and objective of the position: Why does the position exist? Include primary accomplishments, challenges, and products and services related to the position (including who benefits from them and how).

Duties and Responsibilities

- In the order of importance, what are the essential job responsibilities—present and future—needed in order to achieve measurable results?
- What are the daily, weekly, monthly, and annual responsibilities?

- What is the estimated percentage of time spent on each responsibility?
- Describe the authority delegated to this position (including decision-making authority) and note its limits.
- What are the organization's weaknesses (what are the greatest needs)?
- What are the expected deliverables for the first six-to-twelve months?
- Describe the five most important deliverables.
- What are some examples of common and complex problems that this position will be called on to resolve?
- What kinds of issues are typically referred to this position's manager?
- What is the company's direction and how will it affect this position down the road?

Job Qualifications

- What are the minimum requirements necessary to qualify for this position (education, training, special abilities and skills, certifications, licenses, knowledge, experience)?
- What are the specialized/technical skills and knowledge required for this position— now and in the future? (Examples are hands-on industry knowledge, accounting knowledge, including the most current tax laws, P&L responsibilities, Web-based commerce systems, and sales techniques. These skills typically are learned and come from on-the-job work experience, training, and education.)
- What abilities are required above and beyond the learned or technical skills for this position—now and in the future? (These skills are innate strengths of your

candidates. Examples include attention to detail, customer servicing, strategic thinking, relationship building, investigating, and analysis.)

- What characteristics are important to top performance in this position? (Examples: adaptability, analytical ability, assertiveness, detail oriented, collaboration, communication skills, conflict management, creativity, customer service, delegation, follow up, independence, initiative, integrity, interpersonal skills, leadership, listening, negotiation skills, persistence, planning and organizing, problem solving, risk taking, staff development, strategic planning, team building, time management, tolerance for stress, written communications.)
- What differentiates average performers from top performers in this position?
- Identify specialized skills that are essential to carry out the position's responsibilities and make them as specific as possible. Examples include:
  - Interpersonal Skills: interviewing, hiring, coaching, directing, measuring and rewarding performance.
  - Professional/Technical Skills: systems programming, financial analysis, accounting, legal.
  - Managerial Skills: planning, organizing, reviewing, budgeting, directing, taking disciplinary action.
- Describe the company's culture and environment. What characteristics are must-haves for someone to excel and to be self-motivated in this type of environment? (Areas to focus on may include your company's mission and values, marketplace and competition, workflow pace, rules and regulations, communication methods, opportunities for

socializing and risk taking, formal or informal setting, threshold for change, opportunities for collaboration and independent work, hands-on versus hands-off management styles.)

■ Describe the attributes and motivators of the employees who have long tenure and consistent success in similar roles.

■ What are the organizational strengths needed for top performance that the current department may be lacking?

■ What are the greatest challenges and barriers of the job?

■ What personality traits are important for success in this role? (Examples include being self-driven, having a positive outlook, being an empathetic communicator, and eagerness for new experiences and responsibilities.)

Other Physical, Environmental, Mental, and Special Requirements

■ Are there working conditions associated with this position that should be noted (environment, hours, travel requirements, physical demands, etc.)?

■ Describe any unusual or special working conditions.

Other Questions

■ Is this position closely, moderately, or minimally supervised?

■ Does this position have access to confidential information? Please explain.

■ Does this position have access to company funds? Please explain.

■ What is it about working for this company that is most appealing?

- What is the hiring manager's unique management style?
- What are the unique selling points for the open position and company that should be communicated to attract top talent?
- What additional information is relevant to the evaluation of this position?

Phrases for Writing Job Descriptions

Below are sample phrases for each part of the job description. Phrases have been provided for five popular job titles at different position levels: Sales Executive, Administrative Assistant, Chief Financial Officer, Database Administrator, and Product Manager.

Position Purpose

Sales Executive:

- Manages client relationships, implements new product introductions, and assesses client business strategies and needs to increase territory revenue and improve customer satisfaction.
- Maintains and develops territory planning, sales activity, and controls the sales cycle of identified opportunities to achieve sales goals.
- Provides customers with a single point of contact for account management and is responsible for increasing the reach and scope of sales coverage to increase customer satisfaction and drive customer loyalty.
- Responsible for revenue generation and market development of 25 complex accounts with a strong focus

on retention and growth through strategic account planning and execution.

Administrative Assistant:

- Supports multiple executives and a sales team by maintaining files, faxing, copying, coordinating travel, preparing expense reports, planning meetings, and directing telephone calls and visitors.
- Performs a variety of administrative, secretarial, and clerical tasks for the Vice President of Operations. Responsibilities include facilitating systematic and efficient office procedures, and preparing and maintaining records, reports, and confidential files.
- The position of Administrative Assistant assures the delivery of an exemplary level of service to clients and visitors by supervising the concierge team in proper telephone and hospitality skills.

Chief Financial Officer:

- Provides leadership and guidance with respect to the improvement of financial performance of divisional operations. Maintains the integrity of the financial records of the division and has responsibility for the timely and accurate reporting of financial transactions and in forecasting, budgeting, and planning.
- Visionary executive to lead the strategic planning process, develop finance department objectives, and plan, organize, and evaluate financial resources to achieve objectives.
- As a key member of the executive team, the CFO is responsible for all accounting and finance functions,

including plans, policies, practices, budgets, tax, audit, real estate, accounting and insurance, development of business strategies, and takes a leadership role in embracing efficiencies, accuracy, and Sarbanes-Oxley compliance.

- To direct and oversee all financial activities of the corporation, including preparation of current financial reports as well as summaries and forecasts for future business growth and general economic outlook.

Database Administrator:

- Responsible for technical infrastructure support, including relational data warehouse administration and all hardware and software used by database marketing, its internal clients, and external partners.
- Supports the delivery of quality systems by maintaining a stable, reliable environment and comprehensive, high-quality technical support for global relational database systems.
- Maintains site databases and data replication, acts as the point of contact for on-site personnel regarding database administration and replication, implements new databases, and develops and executes implementation plans for new software installations.

Product Manager:

- Guides a team charged with a product line contribution as a business unit. This extends from increasing the profitability of existing products to developing new products for the company.
- Manages a product or product line from concept to final release, maintains product focus and vision, and designs

and coordinates the overall product creation from concept, engineering, marketing, finance, and production before launch.

■ Ensures achievement of strategic revenue objectives for a specific product or product family by playing a proactive role in product planning and design to ensure the product is differentiated from competitors'. Involved with product throughout all stages of life cycle (conception, definition, development, release, and post-release activities).

Duties and Responsibilities

■ List a job description's duties and responsibilities in order of importance.

■ Be brief and include all important duties.

■ Start each statement with an action verb.

■ Indicate the total percentage of time spent on each duty in a typical work cycle (day, week, month, year). Round to the nearest 5 percent. Be sure the total equals 100 percent.

■ If you have someone already doing this job, ask her to delineate her job responsibilities and percentage of time expended. Sometimes the person doing the job will have a different perspective on the job duty priorities and pressures associated with the job.

Sales Executive:

■ Identify and implement products, solutions, and services to customer requirements.

■ Articulate and position a full spectrum of products, services, and solutions to key departmental decision makers.

- Develop and implement business plans for client base to identify, sell, and support incremental value-added services and products in existing accounts.
- Propose and close engagements that will achieve total revenue growth, profit, and customer satisfaction plans.
- Monitor and evaluate progress to ensure achievement of revenue and profit targets.
- Achieve territory sales goals of products, services, and solutions through penetration of large, existing accounts.
- Generate incremental revenue through up-selling and cross-selling activities.
- Prospect and develop relationships with potential customers to qualify and penetrate accounts.
- Sell to "C" level executives to achieve goals and exceed quota responsibility.
- Consistently build and deliver on an accurate account and territory pipeline.
- Effectively communicate to and develop rapport with customers. Evaluate customer's existing and potential product needs and make appropriate recommendations.
- Consistently meet and exceed sales goals as established by local market.
- Generate business through established and creative methods of lead generation.
- Develop and execute events and opportunities to promote and sell products and services to large audiences.
- Implement effective sales closing techniques to ensure product installation goal is achieved.

- Complete associated paperwork, following each customer contact in a timely manner to ensure all details of transaction are completed according to approved and standardized procedures.
- Develop partnership with internal departments to ensure customer satisfaction.
- Stay current on industry trends, best practices, and competition.

Administrative Assistant:

- Identify, classify, maintain, and protect files, documentation, and sensitive information consistent with record handling and retention requirements.
- Type, edit, proofread, and prepare correspondence (e.g., letters, memos, e-mails, responses to requests and inquiries) for internal and external communication.
- Complete and process necessary documents (e.g., expense reports, time cards).
- Maintain department-specific files for easy access and retrieval.
- Review, organize, distribute, and prioritize incoming and outgoing mail.
- Schedule departmental travel arrangements to include air, hotel, and ground transportation.
- Answer and handle all incoming phone calls.
- Transcribe messages and meeting notes from Dictaphone, voice mail, and flip charts for future reference.
- Maintain calendar for department heads.
- Seek out new learning opportunities to enhance job performance.

- Receive and review highly time-sensitive correspondence for company officers. Maintain confidentiality and recommend actions required.
- Screen telephone calls and visitors and resolve routine and complex inquiries.
- Supervise a group of nonexempt secretary staff, including hiring, training, and development.
- Operate a variety of office equipment such as computer, printer, photocopier, transcriber, facsimile, scanner, and calculator.

Chief Financial Officer:

- Oversee financial policymaking and participate in defining the strategies and tactics necessary in achieving company vision.
- Develop financial policies and procedures that ensure complete, accurate, and timely financial and regulatory reporting.
- Develop and maintain enhanced management reporting to facilitate decision making by business units.
- Maintain, develop, and mentor a team of financial professionals.
- Direct the preparation of all financial reports, including income statements, balance sheets, reports to shareholders, tax returns, and reports for government regulatory agencies.
- Oversee accounting departments, budget preparation, and audit functions. Meet regularly with department heads to keep informed and to offer direction.

Developing a Hiring Game Plan

- Review reports to analyze projections of sales and profit against actual figures, budgeted expenses against final totals, and suggest methods of improving the planning process as appropriate.
- Analyze company operations to pinpoint opportunities and areas that need to be reorganized, downsized, or eliminated.
- Confer with President, Vice President of Sales, Vice President of Manufacturing, and division leaders to coordinate and prioritize planning.
- Study long-range economic trends and project company prospects for future growth in overall sales and market share, opportunities for acquisitions or expansion into new product areas. Estimate requirements for capital, land, buildings, and an increase in the workforce.
- Supervise investment of funds; work with banks and/or investment bankers to raise additional capital as required for expansion.
- Oversee financial policies and procedures for the accurate and consistent recording and reporting of all financial matters, including budgeting, external financial reporting, internal financial reporting, restricted grant analysis, capital funds tracking, project cost accounting, project and operational performance analysis, periodic reports to the Board of Directors, internal cost studies, and grant applications.
- Support project activities by establishing guidelines for capital funds utilization and solicitation plus monitoring use of fund/balances, forecasting funds availability, advising on grant/loan usage decisions, and providing project bridge financing/advice to Regional Directors and project staff.

- Oversee investing surplus and unutilized funds to best advantage, and maintain excellent reputation in the financial and fund-granting marketplace.
- Direct special analyses and request special reports in support of project activities, such as tax benefit analyses and financial reporting on use of grant funds.
- Initiate and maintain relationships with major lenders and other providers of capital.
- Participate in long-range and annual development (fund-raising) planning.
- Oversee and direct the Information Services Department, including the establishment of a long-range strategy and execution of yearly plan.
- Support annual budgeting and action planning process.
- Ensure that regional staffing is in place to support financial management responsibilities.
- Direct regional and departmental periodic reporting of actual financial performance against budget and evaluation of variances.
- Provide policies, standards, and guidelines for budgets in grant applications and help provide support for financial reports to grantors.
- Make financial presentations at board meetings and at the periodic meetings of various advisory councils and volunteer groups.
- Supervise and provide leadership to finance department staff of 18 positions, IT department of 10 positions, and regional finance staff.

Database Administrator:

- Provide general administration on database systems, which includes maintaining data stores, schema objects, security and access privileges, software installation and configuration.
- Design, implement, maintain, and automate the appropriate backup and recovery architecture required.
- Implement database replication for reporting and failover purposes.
- Interface with application owners to resolve technical and business issues for which databases could be part of the solution.
- Optimize performance on database and applications.
- Perform capacity planning exercises to properly identify required hardware, software, database configuration/architecture necessary to support application need.
- Implement monitoring, auditing, and alert systems.
- Responsible for physical database design, implementation and support on specific database technologies. Design and implement backup, recovery, archiving, and conversion strategies.
- Identify innovative, cost-effective ways to implement and support physical database technologies.
- Develop staff to assure replacements are in place.
- Provide or recommend required training programs for developing appropriate skills within database technologies. Perform administrative functions related to database support and project activities.
- Establish activity and project timetables.

- Initiate activities and projects related to areas of responsibility.
- Provide ongoing support and enhancements to existing database systems that facilitate current business initiatives.
- Maintain high availability, reliability, and integrity of all database environments.
- Proactively monitor the database to minimize customer impacting situations.
- Support the analysis, design, and implementation of enhancements to existing applications as required and appropriate.

Product Manager:

- Translate market needs into clearly defined and detailed product requirements.
- Team with Sales, Service, Marketing, Product Development, and Product Management to define, develop, market, sell, and deliver the product and the product value proposition in accordance with the Phase Review Process.
- Evolve current integration capabilities to become an industry leader in this area.
- Partner with Product Development to communicate product requirements and determine viable development strategies, deliverables, and release dates.
- Team with Product Marketing, Product Development, Sales, and Service to maintain oversight and shepherd the product (or components thereof) through the Phase Review Life Cycle.
- Maintain understanding of key market drivers, issues, and players in assigned markets.

- Provide regular and detailed communications of product and market status and changes.
- Provide quality, written content into Product Requirement Documentation.
- Provide product-specific support to Sales, Marketing, Professional Services, and Training teams.
- Evaluate competitive market offerings and deliver on differentiation and analysis studies, positioning and communications.
- Maintain a strong understanding of customer needs, industry trends, competitive landscape, regulatory environment, emerging customer segments, and market opportunities.
- Collaborate on proposals, RFP responses, site visits, demonstrations, seminars, and trade shows to support sales efforts.
- Develop high-level business requirements that support services and solutions, in alignment with the corporate business plan.

Job Qualifications

Remember to outline the minimum requirements necessary and focus on technical skills and knowledge, educational degrees, years of experience in a field, performance skills, and personal qualities needed to excel in the job.

Sales Executive:

- Bachelor's degree in business, sales/marketing or related field, or equivalent job related experience.

- Previous outside direct sales experience, software sales experience required (5 years).
- Business background with basic understanding of ROI, financial statement analysis, and accounting concepts/terminology desired.
- Strong organizational, analytical, and administrative and follow-up skills.
- Ability to make 75-plus phone calls per day.
- Must have experience with computer skills in regards to the Microsoft Suite of software and comfort in working with new software applications.
- Strong interpersonal, relationship building, and communication skills.
- Experience in selling consulting services and software solutions.
- Experience in developing new business with large enterprises (Fortune 500, Global 2000) in the United States.
- An understanding of enterprise software solutions.
- Strong writing skills, especially with respect to responding to requests for proposals.
- Willingness to travel.
- Minimum three years of relevant industry and sales experience.
- Ability to handle aggressive targets and pressure.

Administrative Assistant:

- Five-to-seven years experience as an Executive Administrative Assistant providing support to a senior executive in a fast-paced, dynamic environment required.

- Expert with PowerPoint and the creation of advanced presentations.
- Advanced PC skills (proficient using Microsoft Windows, Word, Excel, Outlook, and the Internet).
- Excellent interpersonal and communication skills (written and verbal).
- Excellent analytic, problem-solving, and organizational abilities.
- Ability to handle multiple tasks, projects, competing priorities, and tight deadlines simultaneously while maintaining quality.
- Strong adaptability, flexibility, and resourcefulness.
- Ability to exercise independent judgment and make decisions.
- Demonstrated ability to maintain a high level of professionalism and confidentiality.
- Experience working with international offices and business partners preferred.

Chief Financial Officer:

- Fifteen years (or more) experience as a financial executive.
- Significant investor relations experience, including developing and maintaining relationships within the financial community.
- A strong background working for technology companies, with semiconductor experience of added benefit.
- A degree in a finance-related field accompanied with the ability to offer a broad financial perspective. A CPA is preferred.

- Proven experience building best-in-class planning, reporting, and control functions in an international manufacturing and intellectual property environment.
- Expertise in compliance with SEC and Sarbanes-Oxley regulations.
- Prior success in building and leading high-performance administrative and operations teams.
- Outstanding presentation skills and interpersonal, written, and verbal communication skills.
- Team focus with the ability to motivate others.
- MBA or equivalent degree required.
- Five years of experience in a senior financial management role in a sophisticated and complex financial environment.
- Ten years of experience in increasingly responsible financial positions encompassing a broad range of managerial roles.
- Experience with, and/or understanding of, the special requirements of operating in a not-for-profit business setting.
- Superior leadership, management, and interpersonal skills.

Database Administrator:

- Bachelor's degree in computer science, information systems, or equivalent experience.
- At least three years of industry SAP/Basic Administration experience in a UNIX environment.
- At least two years of database administration experience.
- Ability to provide 24X7 pager and/or on-site support.
- Must be very organized, proactive, and self-directed; able to perform with minimal supervision.

- Must have very strong abstract thinking and problem-solving skills.
- Must have very good verbal and written communication skills.
- Experience with full software development life cycle (SDLC) and methodologies and project and resources management.

Product Manager:

- Strong experience (five years minimum) in product management.
- Strategic and dynamic thinker who can translate business needs into product strategies.
- Understanding of the delivery of health-care business services.
- Strong planning, organizing, prioritizing, and analytical skills.
- Excellent communication skills to both technical and nontechnical audiences.
- Excellent written and verbal skills.
- Ability to work in a fast-paced environment.
- Three-plus years of software marketing/product management experience.
- Ability to be detail-oriented, flexible, self-motivated, and be able to motivate others.
- Must have bachelor's degree. Advanced degree preferred.
- Superior presentation and communication skills, both written and oral.
- Experience with marketing of commercial software, especially within the education industry.

- Strong project management and coordination skills, and ability to excel in a fluid, cross-functional team environment.
- Ability to develop, understand, and apply use-cases to support decision making.
- Previous Web site strategic development experience a plus.

Physical and Mental Demands

List the physical demands that are required for performing the essential job functions. Examples include bending at the waist, crouching, kneeling, crawling, climbing, balancing, lifting, carrying, pushing, pulling, reaching, twisting, writing, squatting, driving, sitting or standing (particularly for long periods of time), and handling (holding, grasping, turning, or otherwise working with the hand or hands). Also list any mental demands that are required to perform the essential functions. Mental demands are not only learned mental skills, but also conditions that call for mental discipline. Examples include reading (documents or instruments), performing detailed work, confidentiality, problem solving, language, stress, training, math, reasoning, oral communication, written communication, customer contact, and multiple concurrent tasks.

- Usual office environment where employee may frequently lift or carry large, heavy, or cumbersome office-related materials up to 50 pounds, or may stand for long periods.
- Non-office environment where employee is required to do the following physical activities (enter crawl spaces, climb ladders, etc.).
- Other unusual physical demands (extraordinary heavy travel).

■ Must be able to concentrate mind and eyes closely on work for sustained periods.

Conclusion

As you define your ideal candidate, keep the following points in mind:

■ When going through the exercises outlined in this chapter, you may find your open position requires an excessive amount of diverse skills. If that's the case, be prepared to conduct a second review to make sure the needs you listed are realistic. Looking for the impossible may dramatically prolong your search.

■ Most human beings tend to be expert in only a few areas and not across the board.

■ You might want to consider realigning your organization so that all your requirements can be met by several employees with the particular strengths and skills your department needs.

■ Avoid the trap of overqualifying your requirements, and thus raising unrealistic standards. This action can be just as dangerous as not defining your job requirements at all, and may lead to hiring overqualified candidates who are under-challenged and underpaid, resulting in future employee retention problems.

■ In some instances, utilizing an assessment tool can help define the right skills and complement to your group. Assessments can help you identify common success factors among those who are currently doing the job and can identify gaps in team productivity, emphasizing areas a new hire could focus on to fill those gaps.

- It's important to keep the job description dynamic, functional, and current so it can effectively be used for conducting future job evaluations. Defining what you are looking for will dramatically help you in your recruiting efforts where targeting the right audience of qualified candidates is key (Chapter 2 will discuss this next step of candidate targeting strategies).

Chapter 2

Find and Attract the Right Talent

Target the Right Candidate

After you have clarified the right job profile and the type of person you think will fill your position, it is time to determine where the right candidate is. There are two types of candidates: the active job seeker and the passive candidate. The active job seeker is a person who has made a conscious decision to actively pursue another position, whether he is presently employed, unemployed, or recently graduated and seeking his first career position. The passive candidate is much more elusive and perhaps the most attractive, because typically that person is gainfully employed and doing a good job with little time to explore outside job opportunities. Recent surveys show that more than 80 percent of people currently employed are passive candidates who would explore an opportunity if they knew it existed and if it was easy for them to access information about the position without jeopardizing their current employment status.

Before setting out after your ideal candidate, consider the following questions:

- What companies would currently employ my ideal candidate?

- Is the ideal candidate in my local market, or will I need to relocate someone from another city?
- What professional organizations would my candidate belong to?
- What conferences or trade shows would she attend?
- What certification or training programs would she pursue?
- What industry publications does she read (newspapers, trade journals, professional newsletters)?
- What Web sites or blogs would my candidate visit on a regular basis?
- Are there any other places that the ideal candidate would congregate, like a local alumni chapter meeting, a diversity organization networking event, a church, civic, or sports-oriented gathering?

Web sites can help you track down organizations, trade associations, or conferences pertinent to your job opening. Check out:

www.weddles.com/associations/index.cfm
www.allconferences.com
www.tsnn.com

Write Compelling Advertising Copy

Whether it is an active job seeker or passive candidate you seek, whether you're advertising in local newspapers or on the Internet, effective exposure of your opportunity to your target market is essential. This means good strategic thinking about where to post your advertisements, but most important it means crafting and communicating a compelling message about why someone would want to work for your company. Perfecting the right phrases in a recruitment advertisement is the key to getting the right attention in a competitive market.

Read the two job postings on page 38 that are for the same job. Which advertisement would you respond to first?

You are probably saying the posting on the bottom is much more compelling, but why? The ad on the top has all of the basic ingredients, but it is not very expressive. Using perfect phrases that illustrate the type of person you seek and colorful adjectives and action words are what make the ad on the bottom stand out. The phrases "superior communications," "highly visible," "due to continued growth," and "most important is your enthusiastic attitude" paint a picture of the position and the type person that appeals to this company.

Here are more perfect phrases that create compelling ad copy.

In this position you will…

- Assume a significant role
- Assume a key role
- Assume a pivotal role
- Assume a leadership role
- Take the lead
- Assume the role of…
- Use your expertise as a…
- Create a new business process
- Lead the initiative to…
- Participate and be a key player on the team
- Report directly to the president
- Become a vital member of our team
- Use your superior project management skills

Sample Ad Copy

Customer Service Representative

Call Center headquartered in St. Louis seeks an experienced customer service representative to handle front line order inquiries in a timely and responsive manner. Strong communication and follow-up skills are very important. Advancement potential, along with good starting salary.

Please send your résumé and salary requirements to Recruiter, P.O. Box 0129, St. Louis, MO XXXXX.

Customer Service Associate

Use your superior communications skills and timely responsiveness to your customers in this highly visible position within our company. Due to continued growth, Hawke-Sloane, one of the nation's largest catalogue home accessories companies, is currently seeking an energetic and outgoing individual to join our team of Customer Service Associates. In this position, you will answer customer inquiries regarding catalogue sales to include tracking shipments, handling change orders, and resolving logistics issues. The ideal candidate should have two – three years customer service experience in a call center environment. Most important is your enthusiastic attitude along with your attention to detail. For the right person, we are willing to offer a good starting salary and benefits, company training, and potential for advancement. For immediate consideration, please contact Julie Anderson at 800-555-1234, or e-mail at jandersen@hawke-sloane.com

Please visit our Web site at www.hawke-sloane.com

We are an Equal Opportunity Employer.

Developing a Hiring Game Plan

- Use your excellent communications skills
- Use your creative talent
- Use your enthusiastic attitude
- Use your high level of initiative
- Use your business acumen
- Use your finely tuned business development skills
- Use your demonstrated sales ability
- Orchestrate a new initiative
- Architect the plan to…

This position offers…

- High visibility
- Growth potential
- Advanced training
- Diversified responsibilities
- Opportunity to interface with…
- Advancement to a leadership role
- A newly created opportunity
- Opportunity to expand your…
- Global responsibilities
- A unique career opportunity to…
- Outstanding benefits to include…
- A ground-floor opportunity
- Excellent base salary
- Generous compensation
- Lucrative commission plan
- Performance based incentives
- Opportunity to deal with top executives

Our company…

- Is the fastest growing in…
- Is one of the fastest growing in…
- Has been recognized as…
- Is one of the largest…
- Is the world's…
- Is the nation's…
- Has a unique working environment
- Prides itself on its…

The ideal candidate should have…

- High level of energy
- Extraordinary ability to relate to people
- Ability to build strong relationships
- Demonstrated background of…
- Track record of success
- Be considered a thought leader
- A strong academic background
- A results-oriented attitude
- A positive attitude
- Confidence in his ability to…
- An attention to detail

It is an aggressive market, and when trying to find great talent it is necessary to stand out from all of the other ads and be easily accessible to the passive candidate. Did you know that on one of the major job boards, there were over 1,000 customer service ads like the ones we showed in our example? A passive candidate won't go to a lot of trouble to get to you because she doesn't have to. Use some of these often overlooked tips to increase your chances of getting good, qualified candidates interested in your opportunity and willing to take the time to respond:

- Use the identity of the company whenever possible so that potential candidates can do their homework on the Internet and become more informed candidates.
- Use a contact name to give some personality behind the person receiving your résumé.
- Make it easy for the candidate to contact you by offering a telephone number as well as an e-mail or fax number to make contact with you.
- Look at your competitors' Web sites to see if they are advertising for the same type of position as you, and note how their postings read.

Many times the best candidates are busy working and don't have an up-to-date résumé. Make it easy for them to make a "curiosity call" to you or your assistant to check out the opportunity firsthand. You might be surprised at how many "passive" candidates call to say that the ad they saw jumped out at them. Your job posting may sound appealing, but many passive candidates will want to know more before they take time from their job to update their résumé.

Data Mining

It's one thing to advertise and wait for someone to respond to your perfect phrases, but reactive recruiting should be balanced with proactive recruiting to the passive candidate market. Data mining is the proactive approach that smart companies are taking to find candidates who may post their résumé but do not search job postings. This takes time and patience, but you can reap huge benefits if you take this step.

In order to do this effectively, it is important to use keyword phrases that will link up to the résumés that are posted and won't totally overwhelm you with thousands of résumés to review. The more specific the words and phrases you use, the better the chances of filtering out those candidates who don't have the basic skill set that you need. Here is where you need to determine hard skills versus soft skills.

Hard skills are those skills or experiences that are tangible and required in order to do the job, such as:

- Microsoft Certified Systems Administrator (MCSA)
- Two years sales experience in merchant credit card sales
- Degree in electrical engineering
- Degree in accounting/finance with a CPA
- IPO experience
- Six Sigma

There is no fudge factor here: These are the minimum skills necessary or the candidate cannot do the job. However, you can consider whether you are willing to accept transferable or easily ramped-up skills, such as:

- Sitting for the CPA exam in the next month versus having already obtained a CPA designation
- Five years business-to-business sales experience including selling cash registers to retailers versus two years of sales experience in merchant credit card sales

Soft skills are more subjective and the level of excellence is judged by the interviewer through the candidate's behavior and past evidence. Soft skills include:

- Superior communications skills
- Strong interpersonal skills
- Flexible nature
- Team player
- Strong business acumen
- Highly motivated
- Demonstrated leadership ability

When data mining, you will notice that most Web sites have some common denominators such as using a keyword search. Use hard skills for your keywords to drill down to the top candidates. Be sure to spell out your requirements completely *and* use acronyms where they may be used, such as Microsoft Certified Systems Administrator (MCSA). When using slashes between words, put a space on either side of the slash, or the key word match must be exact. (Example: project manager / team leader) Other differentiators might be location and salary range.

Target Professional Associations

There are probably professional associations for every occupation, every industry, and every educational background. These associations organize conferences, trade shows, conventions, training and certification programs, newsletters, and career Web sites. Not only can you access their main Web site, but you can also contact the organization directly to ask how you can post or advertise a career opportunity. Direct your inquiry to the Executive Director or the person who coordinates career opportunity advertising. Here are some phrases to use when contacting a professional association:

- "Hello, I would like to inquire about how to advertise a career opportunity."
- "If we post an ad on your Web site, is there a cost involved? How long will it remain on your Web site?"
- "Can we search your membership list or résumé database? Is there a separate charge for that?"
- "Do you know when and where your next [event/conference/trade show/certification training] is being held? Would it be appropriate to advertise our job openings at that event? Is there a résumé exchange area at the event?"

Network for the Right Candidate

Networking is a two-way street. It is also the best way to find employees for your company. Many companies have implemented an employee referral program where employees are motivated to refer friends, colleagues, and external business contacts to their company for open positions. Motivation to the referring employee can be through recognition programs and generous incentives like cash bonuses or gift certificates. Of course, the best situation is when the culture and work environment sells itself through what your employees say about the company. It is always wise to give your employees bragging rights and talking points to spread around the business community.

- "This year our company will take an active part in our industry association by becoming a sponsor for our annual convention."
- "Our company was just recognized as being one of the top 100 growing companies in our city."
- "Our CEO was just honored by the Chamber of Commerce for being voted 'Leader of the Year.'"
- "This year we are having a dynamite holiday party at [venue]!"
- "Our company is really growing and there are a lot of job opportunities, if you know of anyone who is looking."

In addition to your entire employee workforce acting as recruiting ambassadors for your company, you should be actively involved in seeking out networking opportunities. Consider any event or external meeting where you may run into prospective candidates. Think of "six degrees of

➡

separation" when talking to someone heavily networked in your industry or skill set. One person can lead you to another, then another, then another, then voila! You have found the right person! Be ready with the perfect phrases to entice someone to explore a job opportunity with your company, or to suggest someone else that he knows who could be a good fit.

- *Approach a well-networked individual.* "Hi Brad, I thought I might see you here this evening. We have a job opening in our company for a [sales engineer, software developer, administrative assistant, IT consultant, etc.]. I thought with all the people you know, you might know someone who is looking."

- *Approach a person who might know someone to refer, or could be a target candidate themselves.* "Hi Mary, I work for the XYZ Company, and we are looking for a [position] to [join our team, take the lead, take a significant role, etc.]. I thought that you might know of someone that would be interested in talking to us."

- *Direct approach to a target passive candidate. A cup of coffee is a more informal meeting for a passive candidate who hasn't decided yet whether he is interested in exploring another opportunity. This step can help open the door in a noncommittal way.* "Mike, tell me what you do." *Wait for answer.* "That sounds similar to a person we are looking for right now. Maybe we can have a cup of coffee next week and I can tell you more about our open position. It might be of interest to you, or you can tell me where I can find the best people."

➥

■ *Approach to a person who has sent a résumé in, is overqualified for your open position, but may know someone in your industry or skill set.* "John, thank you for sending us your résumé. You have a terrific background, but this position might be less challenging than what you have been used to. I would like to keep your résumé on file, as we may have other opportunities coming up that would be a better fit for your experience level. In the meantime, would you know of anyone you could recommend for this more junior level job?"

Recruit from a Competitor

Recruiting from a competitor is always a little dicey, as most employers are on the lookout for recruiters poaching for their direct competitors. This may be an activity you want to leave to the recruiting pros, as they are in the business of making direct contact with your competition as a normal course of business. There may be ethical considerations in your specific industry or profession that might preclude you from making direct recruiting initiatives into your competition. If, however, you choose to recruit from your competitor or any company in a similar business, here are some professional phrases to use:

- *Calling a person who was referred from a colleague.* "Hi Carol, my name is _____, and Ralph Thomas suggested that I get in touch with you. I am looking for a person to join our software development team, and Ralph thought you might know of someone. Is this a good time to talk?"

- *Calling a person with no referral.* "Hi Bob, my name is _____, and I head up the Software Development team here at _____ and I had heard how connected you are with developers, particularly in the _____ industry. I thought you might know of someone who would be interested in an opportunity we have here in our company?" *If you have reached the head of the company or department, turn your inquiry to this:* "I was hoping that you might have been approached by a candidate when you didn't have a current opening. If you have *any* candidates you can't use, we sure would appreciate the referrals."

- *Direct recruiting call.* "Hi Jerry, I was interviewing a person the other day who suggested that I call you because you might be interested in an opportunity at our company. We are looking for someone to take a pivotal role in our corporate communications department. I'd love to talk to you about it, and wondered if this is a good time." *If he asks you who referred him.* "Well, I keep all people I interview in total confidence. I don't think he wants people to know that he is looking."

Prepare a College Recruitment Program

Many employers choose to develop an effective college recruiting program to train and groom high-potential individuals into their business and their culture. Many schools offer on-site college recruiting career programs where employers can sign up to participate. These career programs usually offer a venue where employers can interview several candidates in a short period of time and have the opportunity to share career information to graduating students.

When developing a program to target college graduates, consider which type of graduate you're targeting and use appropriate recruiting phrases.

College graduate from a four-year college or university obtaining an undergraduate degree.

- "I see you majored in _____. What motivated you to pursue that major and what career path did you think it would afford you?" *Shows insightfulness to connect that specialty to career options.*
- "Tell me about the type of extracurricular activities you have been involved with." *Shows time-management abilities.*
- "Have you ever held any elected offices and if so, how did you achieve that?" *Shows leadership ability and how her peers think about her.*
- "I see where you worked during college. How did you manage that and keep at the top of your class?" *Shows time management and responsibility.*

College graduate obtaining an advanced degree in a master's program awarding a graduate degree, such as an MBA, MS, MA, etc., or a doctorate program awarding a PhD.

- "What made you decide to go into an advanced education program?" *Shows insightfulness.*
- "What [paper, project, dissertation, thesis] are you most proud of and why?" *Showcases accomplishment, preparation, and results.*
- "Have you been involved with any teaching opportunities or new initiatives at your school?" *Shows leadership abilities, dependability, and time management.*
- "What work opportunities have you pursued while working on your [MBA, master's, doctorate, thesis, etc.]?" *Shows multitasking and nonacademic experience.*

Graduate of a technical school obtaining a specific degree based on skills training or certification.

- "What was your most challenging class and why?" *May reveal areas more difficult to learn and how he overcame that.*
- "Did you choose a technical foundation because it comes easy to you?" *Shows an easy ramp-up with short learning curve.*
- "Is there a go-to person in your class who has been helpful in explaining difficult subject matter?" *Shows how to overcome a learning challenge unless, he reveals he is the go-to person.*
- "Have you used your technical proficiency in a work or project setting?" *Shows how she applies skills to a work project, methodology, and processes.*

Chapter 3

How to Choose a Third-Party Recruiter

When Do You Use a Third-Party Recruiter?

Recruiting and interviewing is a very time-consuming process that requires focus. The more recruiting and interviewing you do, the more you will build up your experience level and feel confident in making the right hiring decisions. That said, many times companies seek out help from outside sources to accelerate the recruiting process and to help with sourcing candidates. Here are some of the prime reasons that companies choose to seek outside help:

- Time—Do you lack adequate time to do the proper sourcing and assessment of candidates? If you are doing the screening and interviewing, count on at least 30 to 40 hours dedicated to this task per job opening.
- Expertise—If you are in a tight marketplace with a slim talent pool, you may need outside resources to help tap into databases inaccessible to you to source available talent. Professional recruiters are used to reach out to passive candidates in order to solicit their interest in your position.

■ Objectivity—Many times it is good to have an outside consultant who is in the marketplace every day to offer advice in the hiring decision as you seek out the right hire that will complement your existing staff. Hiring managers who are interviewing for a subordinate or peer level have a tendency to benchmark themselves, which may or may not have the best hiring outcome.

If any of these reasons justify using an outside recruiting service, the next step will be to determine which is the best type of service to use.

Evaluate Service Options

There are many types and levels of service offerings to choose from, along with correlating expenses at each service level. This chapter lists the various categories, their differences, and phrases to use to assess if they are the best fit for your recruiting campaign.

1. *Retainer Search Firms*

As the name implies, these firms require a payment of money up front to retain their search services and are usually reserved for higher-level executive positions. The firm will assign the project to a consultant who will spend time with you and your staff to detail exactly what you are looking for, so that person can create a sourcing strategy for attracting the right candidates. Here are some questions that you might want to ask when screening for the right retainer search firm:

- "Tell me about your firm and how long you have been in the recruiting business." *Probe for their track record and their accomplishments.*

- "Do you specialize in any particular area of recruiting?" *Many firms do specialize in one industry, which has its pros and cons. If a firm specializes in banking, and they have been doing that for 15 years, it is safe to assume that if they are good, they probably have worked with just about every bank in town. If so, where are they going to recruit from: a former or current client? On the other hand, they have a pretty established database of banking candidates and a wealthy networking resource.*

- "Who is the recruiting consultant that we will be working with? What is that person's background?" *You want to know if the consultant has experience within your industry or discipline, or something similar. A professional recruiter can perform her skill in many industries or disciplines. Ask to meet the recruiter prior to engagement, so that you can ascertain how well she has researched 'with' your world.*

- "How many recruiting assignments are you [the recruiter] working on at the present time?" *You want to see if there are too many competing responsibilities that would affect his focus on your particular assignment. Having too many assignments can work against a timely delivery.*

- "How long does it take to begin presenting candidates to us?" *You want to get an idea of the time frame you are dealing with on a normal basis.*

- "Have you worked with any of our competitors before?" *This can be a plus or a minus. You may want to have access to candidates from your competitors and the recruiter may help, but beware of companies that would be eager to recruit from one of their current or former clients. You don't want them to turn around and recruit from you.*

- "How do you source for candidates typically?" *This is one of the greatest benefits you reap from a retained search firm, and you want to know if they have resources, both people and databases, that can help to secure the right talent.*

- "How often do you report back to us your progress?" *Ideally, you would like to have the recruiter in touch with you on a weekly basis to report progress, marketplace issues, relocation or salary issues.*

- "I think it would be a good idea if you can show us some résumés early on so we can make sure we are on track." *Before going too far in the search, it is a good idea to ask for a "temperature check" of any résumés that the recruiter thinks are good, so you can make sure she is hunting in the right direction.*

- "What kind of interviewing do you do, and how do you assess a candidate's fit?" *Thorough interviewing and expert probing of a candidate's background is essential and should require paperwork documentation of interview notes.*

- "Does your company use any assessment tests or tools that can provide a way to ensure the right personality and fit within the company?" *There are a myriad of assessment tools and tests that are used to measure personality and behavior of a candidate that range from online assessments, to handwriting analysis, to in-depth psychological evaluations performed by a professional practitioner.*

- "Are these assessment tests legal to use in making a hiring decision?" *It is important that any of these tests or assessments used have been validated for making hiring decisions and will be used on all final candidates under consideration for the same type of employment. When in doubt check with your internal Human Resources department or externally with an employment lawyer.*

- "How do you check out a candidate's background and past performance?" *You want to make sure that the search firm checks employment and performance references from former employers and gives you written documentation of those conversations. You may also want to contact some of the references yourself to ensure a comfort level in extending an offer to the right person.*

- "How do your fees work?" *Usually a retained search firm will charge on average between 25 percent and 35 percent of annual compensation paid out in thirds, i.e., one-third up front as a retainer, another third after 30 days, and the balance when the candidate is hired. Be prepared that if the entire search takes four to five months, you may be out two-thirds of the fee before anyone is ever hired.*

- "What happens if the candidate does not work out?" *You need to know the guarantee policy of the firm. This is the length of time that the candidate must remain employed with you for them to retain all of their fees, but the policy and length of time may vary from one firm to another.*

- "What is your guarantee period and how does it work?" *Length of time may be from 30 days to an entire year. Policies may include a guarantee to replace the candidate for no additional charge or a refund, which may be the total fee or a portion of the fee.*

- "What happens if we find the candidate on our own while you are searching?" *Most all retained firms will require an exclusive arrangement, that is, regardless of where the candidate comes from, even if it is your son-in-law, you are liable for paying the entire fee. In defense of this, there is the dedicated time the search firm is putting into the search, and the fact they will benchmark this candidate against the rest of the marketplace, so you are ensured you are making the best choice. Exhaust all potential candidates you currently have before entering into an exclusive arrangement.*

- "What is your retention rate of people you place and how do you measure this?" *This can be very telling if they have an exceptionally high retention rate with multiple hires in a year. See if their rates are measured on the guarantee period or for 12 months.*

- "What client references may we contact?" *This is the best way to ensure that you are selecting a firm that has a good reputation for delivering the right candidate.*

- "What type of information do you share with us regarding candidates and companies you have contacted?" *Usually a retained search firm will give you a candidate report of how many people they have contacted and the companies these candidates come from. Do not expect a list of candidates with titles and companies, as this is confidential information.*

Retained search firms can be very expensive, but their thoroughness, due diligence, and sourcing expertise can be a very compelling reason to select this method. Be sure to do *your* due diligence and know who you are dealing with, the length of time they have been in business, and the reputation of the firm.

2. *Contingency Search Firms*

The bulk of recruiting firms have traditionally been contingency search firms whose total fees are contingent upon the successful placement of an appropriate candidate. The advantage is that there is no money at risk up front because you only pay a firm if they fill the open position. The disadvantage is that there is no real commitment from the contingency firm. You don't know how much time is going to be devoted to your project. Here are some questions to help you screen which contingency search firm would be right for you:

- ▪ "Tell me about your firm and what type of positions you work on." *The probe here might not be as extensive as for retainer firms since you have nothing to lose except for banking on a contingency firm that really has no business in your specialty area.*
- ▪ "Are you doing the recruiting or is there another recruiter that will handle my needs?" *Many times there is a salesperson who will make the initial contact and who will pass your information on to a recruiter. It is wise to speak directly to the recruiter to make sure that person understands your job opening.*
- ▪ "Does your recruiter specialize in this specific industry or discipline?" *The advantage of specializing is that the recruiter is well-versed in your business. The disadvantage is that when the recruiter is working with multiple companies at one time it may create more competition for you if the recruiter is working with your competitors at the same time, which prompts another question:* "Are you working currently with any of our competitors for the same type position?"

➡

- "How much time can you devote to my recruiting position a week?" *This is an important evaluator because the recruiter is working on multiple "job orders" at a time, so your recruiting project must fit into that person's workload. Many recruiters are working on 15 to 20 job orders simultaneously, so if you do the math, your job order will get only so many hours per week.*

- "How difficult or challenging do you think this position will be to fill?" *The more difficult or challenging does not guarantee that you will get extra recruiting time. The recruiter may be motivated by commissions for positions filled, so the easiest or fastest to fill get the most attention.*

- "How do you source for the right candidate?" *Most contingency firms will refer to who is in their internal database first before recruiting from target companies. Again, determine how much time the recruiter will have in a week to recruit for passive candidates.*

- "How do your fees work?" *Most contingency firms charge a certain percentage of the annual salary ranging from 20 percent to 30 percent. Expect an invoice when a placement has been filled.*

- "Our company has a policy of not paying more than 15 percent fees. Can you work with this?" *Contingency firms will in many cases negotiate fees depending upon the marketplace, but beware: If your recruiter is motivated by commissionable income based upon the fees, your lower negotiated fee can backfire and result in "adverse selection." The recruiter has an incentive to send the best résumés to the highest paying clients first and your discounted fee may compromise the quality of candidates you see.*

- "Is the salary that we are contemplating competitive with the marketplace?" *Here again, you must ascertain the motivation of the recruiter. If you are paying below market averages, the recruiter who works a particular market may be sending the same résumés at the same time to your higher paying competitor. The recruiter may be motivated to sell the opportunity where there is a greater payout.*

- "We have a recruiting and selection process within our company that typically can take 90 days or more if hiring managers are traveling. Is this a problem?" *To a contingency firm, 90 days is an eternity. Chances are that by the time the recruiting cycle comes to an end, your candidate will have many other options to weigh, creating a more competitive situation.*

- "Do you check references?" *Ask for documentation along with the résumé.*

- "How do you guarantee the candidates you place?" *Refund guarantees rather than replacement guarantees will give you the greater advantage, as you are not sure if the search firm will have the time to dedicate to the project if a replacement is needed.*

- "What is your candidate-placement ratio?" *This is the ratio of open job orders to positions filled. This can give you some idea of how successful the firm is at closing open job orders, and whether or not you will work with several other contingency firms at the same time for your open positions.*

- "What kind of interviewing do you do to assess the candidate?" *Candidate screenings can range from a 15-minute telephone screen to an in-person, hour-long interview. Most interviews will be generic as opposed to specific interviews, based upon your particular job opening situation. Rely upon your own resources for in-depth interviewing and selling the opportunity to the candidate.*

Contingency search firms are a great way to shop the market without a financial or time commitment. You might want to elect to use more than one contingency firm at the same time to spread your position exposure and not have all your eggs in one basket. Just remember that commitment goes both ways, and candidates that you will be seeing will be marketed—at the same time—to companies competing for the same talent. Caution: be careful on entering into an exclusive engagement with a contingency search firm unless you get a satisfactory answer to the question, "What do I get extra as far as time commitment and making my opportunity a top priority with your recruiter?"

3. Contract Recruiter

A newer breed of recruiting practitioner is the freelance recruiting consultant, or contract recruiter . This recruiter typically comes to your place of business to work on your recruiting projects. Fees run the gamut, but typically a contract recruiter is paid by the hour for the time that he is working on your projects, so there is an up-front investment. The advantage is that you are paying for time spent as opposed to paying for each position, so the cost can be much lower than traditional retained or contingency firms. The risk you run is that the contract recruiter may not be able to deliver, and you may pay for several weeks or months of work before you know if he can turn activity into expected outcomes. There is usually no guarantee period for the newly hired, so if the candidate does not work out, the contract recruiter will just have to start the search over again at his hourly rate. Here are some questions to ask if you are interviewing a contract recruiter:

- "What is your recruiting background?" *Probe for specific training and recruiting experience, because each person comes with a different skill set. The contract recruiter may have come from an internal company recruiting environment or an outside search firm environment.*
- *If the recruiter is from a corporate recruiting background:* "What kind of recruiting and candidate sourcing did you do at the _____ corporation?" *If the contract recruiter comes from a corporate background, probe for sourcing techniques in the recruiting process to see if she was on the receiving line of someone else's sourcing, or if she was heavily involved with sourcing herself.*

- *If the recruiter is from a search firm background:* "Why would you want to work in a more corporate recruiting environment as opposed to the search firm environment?" *Most search firms are very pressure intensive with a strong emphasis on results that are well rewarded. If the contract recruiter left that environment, play close attention to why. It may be because it was too pressure oriented, he was not up to par in terms of expected results, or he is seeking something that addresses the full talent management life cycle.*

- "Do you recruit for exempt or nonexempt positions? *Determine up front what level of hiring the contract recruiter is experienced in. The skill level is different for hiring an hourly wage employee rather than a highly skilled professional employee.*

- "What is the most complex/challenging position you have ever recruited for?" *Get some war stories to demonstrate how resourceful your recruiting practitioner is when the going gets tough.*

- "If you have recruited for executives, how does that differ from lower-level professional recruiting?" *Differentiate techniques and steps used to attract and assess top-level executives.*

- "Has your recruiting been on a localized geographic basis, or on a national or international basis?" *Geography has a lot to do with how complex the recruiting project will be. If your recruiting is a national search or you need to fill multiple positions in different cities around the country or the world, make sure the contract recruiter has that specific experience. Ask how she will source candidates outside of her locality.*

- "Do you adhere to any particular recruiting process? If so, describe that process." *Recruiting requires a sequence of steps that changes depending upon the complexity of the project. Visualize how that process will integrate with your company's established policies and availability of hiring managers for the interviewing and selection process.*
- "How many open positions for your client have you recruited for at one time?" *Get an idea of the recruiting volume the contract recruiter has handled if this is important for your needs.*
- "What are your time-to-fill averages?" *It is good to know how many days from start to hire the contract recruiter averages. Forty-five days is a good showing, but it does depend upon how fast the hiring company makes a decision. That may factor outside of the contract recruiter's control, but he should be able to influence the process timeline.*
- "Do you have any sort of database of candidates to work with?" *Is the contract recruiter coming in with an existing database of candidates, or will she be leveraging the company database?*
- "Have you had experience working with an applicant tracking system?" *These are computer systems that track an incoming résumé through to the conclusion of the open position. This usually requires reporting back to the system as you go along, which is another step in the recruiting process requiring administrative detail.*
- "Do you have your own applicant tracking system?" *If your company does not have an applicant tracking system, it could be helpful if the contract recruiter has that capability. This will keep your recruiting records in order.*

- "With your last client, what percentage of positions did you actually fill, and what percentage was worked through other outside search firms or vendors?" *You want to make sure that the contract recruiter has the track record and ability to fill positions on her own, or you might risk paying an hourly fee* and *a placement fee on top of that if you have to resort to using an outside search firm if the job remains unfilled. On the other hand, you might want the contract recruiter to fill a core number of positions and manage a vendor relation with other outside vendors.*

- "Why did you leave your last client? Are they still hiring?"

- "In the last year, how many positions did you recruit for? How many did you fill?" *This will demonstrate recruiting attempts versus actual closed positions.*

- "Do you measure retention rates of candidates you hire?" *This will give you an idea of the quality of hiring that the contract recruiter has done.*

- "Tell me about a candidate that declined the offer at the last minute." *This can be a good gauge to see how well the contract recruiter shepherds the entire process to completion.*

- "What is the most difficult recruiting process you have encountered, and how did you deal with it?" *All recruiters have to work within their client's recruiting process, and some processes are more dysfunctional than others. See what kind of change agent a recruiter may have been to help establish best practices within his client company.*

- "How do you deal with your hiring managers?" *A good recruiter will get the hiring manager engaged and interested in the search process, without grabbing too much time from busy hiring managers.*

➡

- *"Would you rather recruit for technical positions or sales positions?" There are many different approaches to recruiting different types of positions, especially when one type requires assessment of hard/tangible skills and another requires assessment of more soft/intangible skills.*

Going the contract recruiting way may be a good choice if you want a dedicated recruiting resource at an economical rate, but success depends upon the type of recruiting experience the recruiter brings to the table, and how long it will take to ramp up to be effective. Even better is making sure that the recruiter not only understands recruiting, but also understands how this new hire will impact the business.

4. Recruitment Process Outsourcing (RPO)

This is a hybrid of the former three types of recruiting approaches. It combines the thoroughness of the retainer firms, the contingent factor in the fee schedule, and a focused and dedicated approach with consistently trained professional recruiters who work on-site at the client location. An infrastructure of professionals manages the engagement, and sourcing specialists provide support to the on-site recruiters. Typically an RPO arrangement will consist of volume hiring needs, possibly to support multiple locations. Here are some questions to ask a potential RPO vendor:

- "Tell me the background of your company and what type of recruiting engagements you have managed."

- "What kind of profile do you seek in recruiters you hire?" *Does she come from an HR corporate recruiting background or a search firm background? Has she done her own team building before for her own department? Does she understand the business impact of hiring a particular talent beyond understanding a skill set?*

- "What kind of training do you have for your recruiters?" *Is there consistent training for each recruiter that ensures consistent delivery?*

- "Do you deal with full life cycle recruiting?" *Does this span experience from workforce planning, position requisition process, establishing roles and responsibilities, sourcing strategy and execution, candidate assessment and selection, offer process, and onboarding or orientation process?*

- "Do you have a particular methodology?" *Is it based upon a contingency search or a corporate recruiting process? Is*

there a sourcing process? Does he shepherd the candidates throughout the entire hiring process?

- "What kind of applicant tracking system do you have?" *Can it be integrated into your reporting, or can it enhance your reporting? How is the applicant tracking used to help you establish a pipeline of candidates?*
- "Can you integrate your system and process within our existing one?"
- "Can you work on-site with our other core recruiters?" *Is this a collaborative partnership with your other HR employees, or does she want to take over all of the recruiting function?*
- "Is it necessary to outsource our entire recruiting function to your company, or can we select a particular project area?"
- "Can we start with a trial program?" *Would it be advisable to develop a pilot program to work out the kinks before embarking on a long-term contract?*
- "Can you support other geographic locations?" *If you are a national or global company, does this company have the capacity to help you in all your geographic locations?*
- "What metrics or reviews do you provide to us to show your performance?" *How often can you get feedback from the company as to project progress and short-/long-term results?*
- "What is your fee structure and payment terms?" *Is there a retainer component along with a variable component based upon results? It might be more motivating if the recruiter gets some compensation based upon successful delivery.*

Establish Recruiting Parameters, Timelines, Expectations, and Accountability

Now that you have chosen which type of outside recruiting resource you will use, it is up to you to establish the ground rules and make sure that expectations are clearly understood. You should review very carefully any contracts or agreements and the scope of responsibilities. Here are probing questions you should ask any outside company or contractor before entering into a formal engagement.

- "Do you have a standard contract or agreement?"
- "Does your contract spell out your responsibilities and what you need from us?"

   If there is an exclusive component to the contract:
   - "What is the duration of the exclusivity?"
   - "What if we have an internal candidate that crops up?"
   - "We have an internal employee referral program. How would that work with your exclusive arrangement?"

- "Does your contract spell out how long it will take before we see candidates?"

   If there is a retainer component to the contract:
   - "How does the retainer work and when is it due?"
   - "What happens if we don't hire a candidate or like anyone?"

- "Will you meet with our hiring managers personally to discuss the job profile and the current job situation?"
- "Will you meet with our HR team to understand our HR policies?"
- "Will you conduct reference checks on identified candidates?"

- "Does your company perform background, criminal, motor vehicle, credit, and drug testing as part of your service?"
- "What guarantees do you provide if we hire one of your candidates?"
- "Will you provide a detailed pipeline report of candidates that you are recruiting on a weekly basis?"

Negotiating a Reasonable Fee Schedule

Fees for services rendered can sometimes be negotiated. Retainer search firms are usually set in their fees, but may negotiate if the marketplace reflects slow hiring or epidemic layoffs, but those days have basically ended because of the predicted labor shortage as we move through this decade. Remember that negotiating the lowest rate with a contingency search firm may not be the best choice if the recruiter is motivated by commissionable earnings. A contract recruiter's hourly fees are usually up for negotiation, especially if you are dealing with a solo practitioner. RPO types of organizations span from high-volume hiring for hourly wage employees to those that recruit in the professional level. Most fees, howerer, can be negotiated based upon volume of hiring and complexity of hiring. Here are some typical negotiations phrases:

- "Can we expect a reduced fee schedule based upon hiring more than one position, or if we have multiple hiring needs?"
- "Are your fees inclusive of all sourcing costs like advertising, job posting, job board searching?"
- "What if you have to travel to interview candidates or must bring in candidates from out of town?"
- "What are your payment terms? Is your company financially able to sustain [30-/60-/90-day] payment terms, which are normal with our vendors?"
- "What happens to the fees if the candidate does not work out within the guarantee period? Can we get our money back on non-retained work?"

Part Two

Screening, Interviewing, and Evaluating Candidates

Chapter 4

Prescreening Candidates

There are tremendous benefits to prescreening your candidate pool:

- You can focus your efforts on interviewing the right candidates—only those who meet your job specifications—saving you time and enhancing your productivity during the hiring process.
- The more you know about a candidate ahead of time, the better prepared you will be, and you can select appropriate questions accordingly.
- You will be able to narrow your candidate pool down to a manageable level.

In this chapter, we are going to focus on application, résumé, and telephone screening techniques. As in any interview process, screening questions must meet EEOC (Equal Employment Opportunity Commission) regulations, and questions pertaining to the following should be avoided: race, ethnic background or national origin, religion, sexual orientation, marital status, living arrangements, children, health information, and age (unless necessary to prove eligibility of work).

Résumé Screening

The first step to prescreening candidates is to sift through all the résumés you have received. Have your job description handy so you can keep the qualities and skills you are seeking top of mind. There are certain components you should expect to find on most résumés—a candidate's contact information, employment and educational history, including dates, career objectives (this may be in the cover letter), achievements and responsibilities, and career-related affiliations.

Here are some tips to help you effectively sift through your résumés:

- Review them in small doses.
- Sort them into three groups: yes, no, maybe. (You may want to consider marginal candidates if your candidate pool is small. A quick phone call or e-mail may expedite your sorting.)
- Have at least two people review the résumés. A second review can ensure that each résumé gets a fair and complete evaluation.
- Take notes on any concerns such as unexplained gaps in employment and list questions you want to ask during a telephone screen.
- Don't rely solely on technology to screen résumés for key words and phrases (e.g. "PowerPoint" or "budget administration") that describe your desired skills and background. Such programs are useful if you are receiving hundreds or thousands of résumés and you need to filter out unqualified candidates. (If you expect a deluge of résumés and you're willing to lose out on

➡

some potentially strong candidates, this may prove a cost-effective, time-saving step.)

- It's often wise to have a human being devote at least one to two minutes scanning each résumé to get a complete picture of each candidate. You may have the flexibility to hire someone who lacks certain skills but possesses other highly valuable talents that you can use. Moreover, strong applicants can get screened out because their résumé lacks a certain word, even if they're otherwise well qualified.
- Flag achievements and require candidates to elaborate in an interview so that you fully understand their actual roles and responsibilities.
- If you find a candidate who is short in education , for example, but has had similar job experience, don't just eliminate him. The similarity in work experience can make him a credible candidate. Always ask yourself:"Is the candidate doing it? Has he done it? Can he progress into doing it?"

Following is a list of questions that résumé reviewers and screeners should take into consideration when prescreening résumés:

- "Does the résumé seem tailored for the position, or is it a résumé that seems to have been mass mailed?"
- "Does the candidate's qualifications and education meet the minimum requirements for the position?"
- "Has the candidate hopped from job to job, company to company, and school to school?"
- "Which job requirements were not covered in the résumé, and are they areas that can be learned?"

- "Does the résumé demonstrate that the candidate is a self-starter and that she shows future promise and initiative? How has she updated her education and work experiences?"
- "Has the candidate proven competency in the required focus of the job through past experience?"
- "Are all required certifications and licenses listed?"
- "Does the résumé show inconsistencies in formatting, dates, descriptions, titles, responsibilities, and salaries? Is there information for some positions but not others?"
- "Is the résumé believable or does it seem to be padded with unbelievable accomplishments?"
- "Are there gaps of unexplained employment history?"
- "Does the résumé reflect depth and variety of experience?"
- "Is the résumé neat, professional, without typos, well-written, well-organized, and complete?" *Especially critical if you are looking for someone with those abilities and a strong attention to detail.*
- "What is the candidate currently doing?" *Ask during a telephone screen if this is vague or unclear.*
- "Are deficiencies in a candidate's work record covered up by padding the résumé with hobbies, activities, and experiences not related to the position?"
- "Is the résumé in a functional format?" *There are basically two types of résumés—"chronological" and "functional." The mostly widely used is the chronological résumé, which lists employment history in reverse chronological order, from the most recent position to the earliest. The functional résumé emphasizes skills or "functions" and may not even list dates. Even though*

functional résumés have become more popular in recent
years, they may signal that the candidate has something
to hide, especially gaps in employment and experience.
Don't rule these candidates out; just follow up with
questions during a phone screening.

- "Does the candidate seem to take too much credit for projects undertaken by several staff members?"
- "Are vague generalities (e.g. 'worked with legal documents' and 'participated in …') used throughout the résumé or are statements tied to specific end results?" *Watch out for vague responsibilities and claims, and look for specific details of achievements and outcomes. A candidate that "handled invoices" could have simply delivered them from one desk to another. Get specifics.*
- "Does the candidate's career path seem to be inconsistent? Were there a lot of lateral moves, short-term stints, and different professions?" *Keep in mind that in certain professions, job mobility is more of the rule than the exception. Pay attention if someone is in a consulting role and he is on shorter term projects.*
- "Determine the candidate's career patterns. Is there steady progress and promotions in past employment and is there stability, or has the candidate changed jobs every six months?" *Be aware of current economic conditions. During a time of downsizings, lateral career moves may indicate that someone is a survivor and is flexible and can take on new responsibilities and handle change. As a general rule, more time in one place shows loyalty. However, even the best employees can have short periods of employment due to unforeseen and uncontrollable*

➡

circumstances. It's better to hire someone who considers your opening as a strategic career move than someone who is looking for some other reason, like she currently doesn't get along with her boss.

- "Is the candidate an achiever and does he have the bottom line at the top of his mind?" *Look for accomplishment statements that list results and not just responsibilities* (e.g., "Increased revenue 25 percent by …" or "Achieved customer satisfaction scores of 97 percent by …"). *Does the résumé indicate this candidate is budget conscious, profit minded, and successful at reducing costs, for example? The more achievements in a résumé, the more you will want to read further.*

- "Is the candidate's relevant work experience recent or from many years ago?"

- "Is the candidate's most recent title 'consultant' without any mention of specific tasks and results, clients, or company employed with?"

- "Does the résumé contain false or inflated information?" *A misspelled certification acronym may indicate false information or may simply be a typographical error. Look for inflated titles, for example, but consider the fact that companies may themselves inflate titles to boost morale. The key to interpreting an inflated title is to fully understand the role of the job.*

- "Are references provided?" *If so, look at the names and titles. It's a good sign if the résumé gives you former supervisors' names.*

- "Are there indications of problem solving?" *Be sure to ask for descriptions of what the problem was, how it was solved, and the outcomes.*

➡️

- "Are there volunteer activities and leadership roles in other professional and community organizations?" *Indicates motivation, responsibility, and ability to multitask.*
- "Is there a career objective? If so, is it specific or general, and does it match your open position?"
- "Is the résumé longer than the standard one- or two-page résumé? Alternatively, is it too short?" *If so, your candidate might be long-winded or not have enough experience. You'll learn more once you conduct a telephone interview and evaluation.*
- "Did the candidate attend educational institutions with tenuous accreditation? Was the candidate employed by companies with an unsavory reputation? Does the résumé provide information that cannot be verified, such as a professional certification?" *Look for exaggerations, embellishments, and mistruths.*

Just because a résumé has a few gaps doesn't necessarily mean you should overlook it. The key to your success is staying focused on the skills and the value that the candidate can potentially bring to your organization.

Telephone Screening

After you have identified résumés you would like to consider, your next step is to conduct short, 10- to 15-minute telephone screening interviews that will save you time and money in the long run. You are not soliciting in-depth information at this point—you are simply narrowing the field. Your objectives are to:

- Ask questions that were not obvious from the résumé, especially reasons for leaving, gaps in employment, job hopping, and salary history and requirements. Clarify any issues and get a better sense of a candidate's skills and background.
- Appraise the candidate's interpersonal skills, and if the candidate meets your basic screening criteria.
- Determine the candidate's motivation and interest level.
- Determine which candidates best meet your needs and possess the essential qualifications that you want to invest in further with a face-to-face interview.

It's best to prepare a short list of questions to ask each of your candidates and it's important that you gather the same kind of information from each candidate. Define questions that will eliminate candidates from being considered. Elimination questions can be about skills, recent work, or a candidate's ability to work long hours or travel, for example. The following are some examples of elimination questions:

- *If your company isn't paying for relocation.* "We're not paying for relocation expenses. Are you still interested in the position?" or "Are you willing to relocate to Atlanta at your expense?"

- *If travel is a strong requirement.* "This position requires that you travel out-of-state 50 percent of the time. Are you still interested?"
- *You can also use technical elimination questions, for example, if you want to make sure a candidate knows your product.* "How much experience do you have with _____?"

To begin the telephone screen, introduce yourself and ask if this is a convenient time for the candidate to talk for a few minutes. Talk about the company, highlights of the job description, and how you received the candidate's résumé. Toot your company's horn, as you are selling just as much as the candidate. For example:

- "This is a long-established company with a reputation of being top-notch in expertise and service."
- "The company is expanding and offering growth opportunities in career and responsibility. Your position offers high visibility working in a pivotal role where you can really make a difference."
- "You will be working out of the new, state-of-the art headquarters location that is a showplace distribution and training center."

Listen to the way candidates communicate and ask questions around critical skills you are looking for.

If the candidate isn't available, leave a message with a specific time for when he or she should return your call. This can be a good test of initiative. Candidates who do not return the call by the designated hour to make alternative arrangements may demonstrate a lack of interest or

➡

commitment. Some common questions to ask during a telephone screening include:

- "Why do you want to leave your present company?" or "Why are you interested in leaving your current position?" or "Why do you want to make a change?"
- "Tell me about your background—accomplishments and goals."
- "What are you currently doing and what did you do before that?"
- "What kind of [state functions/skills looking for] experience do you have?"
- "Please tell me about your employment experience," or "Could you give me a recap of your work experience?"
- "What makes this position attractive to you? Describe your qualifications as they apply to this position."
- "Describe your most successful accomplishments."
- "What do you like and dislike about your current position?"
- "When are you available to start?"
- "Are you willing to relocate?"
- "Do you have any questions about the position that I may answer for you?"
- "I'd like to hear more about your background working with [customers, budgets, etc.]."
- "What type of work are you looking for?"
- "Based on my brief description of the job, what is your level of interest in it?"
- "What do you know about our company?"
- "Why do you think you would fit into our company?"
- "What is your current salary, and what are your salary expectations?" or "What salary range are you expecting?"

➡

Sometimes candidates are coached not to provide the answer. Here are some key phrases that you can use to solicit salary information:

- "Salary is somewhat open to the candidate with the right background and skills. I want to see if we are in striking distance." *If the candidate is in the ballpark, tell him.*

- *If he asks you what the position offers.* "I'm unable to share salary right now. I can share further in the process."

- *If there is a bonus.* "What are you looking at for the year's total and what did you make last year in bonuses? I need to know for us to move forward."

- "Have you managed others? How many individuals have you managed at one time?"

- "Have you ever managed employees in a union environment?"

- "Are you bilingual?"

- "Can you tell me about your current job?"

- "What sort of work environment brings out your best performance?"

- *Develop a question that will assess the experience of the candidate.* For example, "How many years of sales management experience do you have?"

- *Develop a question that will assess the experience of the candidate specific to your needs.* For example, "Tell me about your experience with managing strategic accounts."

- "Are you willing to have a drug test, a criminal background check, reference checks, educational

➥

background checks, and others as appropriate for this position?"

- *If the candidate is not currently working.* "Why and when did you leave your most recent position? How have you spent your time since you left?"

Opening phrases:

"Hello. May I speak with [candidate's name]? This is Wendy Harris from Hawk-Sloane. I am in receipt of your résumé for the Vice President of Retail Operations position and I wanted to briefly discuss the opportunity with you. Do you have about 10 minutes to speak with me now or should we schedule a more convenient time for you?

Next, briefly discuss the company and position highlights to get the candidate excited:

"We are one of the Southeast's most well-established and highly branded retailers with over 150 retail locations throughout the Southeast. We currently have over 1,000 employees and we are in an expansion mode, which is why we are looking to fill this newly created position. This position will be reporting directly to the company president, so there is a lot of visibility in this very pivotal position. You would be overseeing the entire retail operation, including all expansion activities, and there are approximately 60 district managers that would report to you. How does that sound so far?" *Evaluate the candidate's interest level.*

Then gather additional information about the candidate:
"I just have a few questions …

- What are you currently doing now?
- What is it that has prompted you to look for a new opportunity?

- What did you do prior to your current position?
- Describe for me your retail operations experience.
- Give me a specific example of when you developed and implemented initiatives that significantly enhanced the customer experience. What did you specifically do and what was the outcome?
- Describe your experience in developing store layout and merchandising guidelines.
- What aspects of your current (or last) position did you like the most/least?
- What are you looking for in your next opportunity?
- Are you able to travel over 50 percent out-of-state?
- Are you open to relocation?
- What is your current salary arrangement?
- Do you have any questions?"

To end the phone screen:

- *If the candidate isn't a good fit.* "We have other candidates who appear to have credentials and experience that more closely match the expectations of the position."
- *If the position is too senior.* "This position is a bit senior. You have a great background and we will retain your information if something else should come up. If you know anyone that may have more senior experience, we would welcome referrals." *Do the same if the person is overqualified and you need someone more junior.*
- *If you have a candidate who fits.* "What is your time frame? Can we schedule an in-person interview?"
- *If you're not sure at the end of the telephone screen if you want this candidate to move to your short list.* "I am in the beginning stages of the interviewing process and I have

a lot of other candidates to speak with at this point. If you are still interested in the position, write me a letter or send an e-mail that details how your specific background and accomplishments match each requirement from the job description." *This additional step may help you evaluate the candidate's motivation and written communication skills.*

For candidates who seem like a good fit, schedule the in-person interview at the end of the phone screen for maximum efficiency. Once you have several high-quality candidates scheduled for the next step, you are ready to conduct face-to-face interview sessions.

Application Screening

It's prudent to have qualified candidates fill out an employment application when they come in to your office location for an interview. Compare applications to a candidate's résumé, as it can give you a more accurate picture of that person's history (an application will generally contain information not typically found on the résumé). You can also look for sloppiness and inconsistencies, as applications are handwritten. Employment applications request accuracy and truthfulness, and they generally include a statement that reads, "I understand that false or misleading information may result in termination of employment." Applications ask candidates for specific information including:

- Contact information
- Work experience
- Education
- Salary history
- Desired times of work (full-time or part-time)
- Special skills and awards
- Names and contact information of former supervisors to check as references
- Current employment status
- Permission to contact current employer
- Criminal convictions
- Reasons for leaving previous employers
- Eligibility to work in the United States

Chapter 5

Conduct a Productive Interview

Set Up an Interview

As mentioned in Chapter 4, for maximum efficiency it is best to set up an interview right away during a telephone screen when you have concluded that the candidate has met the minimum requirements. You may be very excited about the candidate, especially in a tight market, and it is okay to be enthusiastic about the upcoming meeting, but you don't want to sound desperate. Remember that time is of the essence and you want to get the candidate in for an interview as soon as possible. The longer you wait to have an interview, the more chances you have of losing a great candidate in a tight job market. This is truly a case of "if you snooze, you lose." Here are some perfect phrases for scheduling and planning an interview:

- "[Candidate], I think it would be a good idea for us to get together and discuss in more depth the position we have open here. What is your availability for an interview this week?"
- "[Candidate], your background with the [XYZ Company] seems to have a lot of similarity to what we are looking for. Does this seem to be of interest to you?" *If so* ... "Let's go ahead and set up a time for us to get together."

- "[Candidate], have you had a chance to look at our Web site and do you have any questions?" *Assuming a positive exchange...* "I believe our next step should be to get together for an interview time where we can exchange a lot more information and see if this is a good fit for us both."

- "We should allow at least [length of time] for an interview." *You should allow ample time for your interview so it will not be rushed. For any professional-level position, allow a minimum of one hour for a first interview. Be respectful of any working candidates so that they can return to work and not endanger their current job. If your candidate is traveling in from another city, you might want to maximize the time and cost by having him meet with any other hiring decision-makers on the same day.*

- If you are playing telephone tag, or e-mailing an exchange. "Hi [Candidate], I thought we should go ahead and set up a time to get together about our open position. Here are some of my available times this week [dates/times]. Let me know what might work for you." *Don't list more than two or three choices. You might want to make one time very early or after work, if your candidate is currently working. Be respectful of the fact your working candidates have responsibilities to meet.*

- *Always give excellent directions. Nothing is more disconcerting to a candidate than to get lost and be late for an interview.* "[Candidate], let me make sure you know how to get here. If you get lost, please call me at this number [phone number], or call the front desk at [phone number] if you have any difficulty. *It is a good idea to have directions to your company printed and on file to fax or e-mail to a candidate.*

- *If a candidate is traveling into town for an interview, nothing is more important than the entire candidate experience. Have a well-planned itinerary, including all ground transportation. Don't assume your out-of-town candidate has any knowledge of your city, including traffic patterns or local landmarks.*
  - "We will be making your flight reservations and will get to you [the travel documents/confirmation number/rental car information/ground transportation instructions] . If you have any problems, please contact me or my assistant at [telephone number]. We look forward to seeing you on [date]."
  - "Please make your own travel arrangements and keep an expense record, so that we can reimburse you when you are here. We expect to pay for a coach flight, lodging at [a business hotel/a specific hotel], your [rental car/taxi/ground transportation/parking], and [your meals while you are here/per diem money for meals]."

Prepare for the Interview

Before you have an actual interview, it is important to prepare for it. Know what you are trying to accomplish: finding the person who can do the job, and who will become a valued asset to the organization. Take your job description out and put the following requirements in column form to be your guidepost as you interview:

- the minimum experience, background, or education required
- the preferred experience or background
- the personality characteristics required

Read the candidate's résumé from beginning to end and make notes of questions you have on a separate piece of paper. These questions should help clarify how well the candidate matches your job requirements and will help you to remember what areas to probe. While perusing the résumé, ask yourself:

- "Are there any gaps in employment?"
- "Does the educational background specify a degree received?"
- "Do the titles on the résumé make sense in a career progression, or does the career seem to regress?"
- "If there are a lot of jobs listed, is there a valid reason?"
- "If the candidate has been a manager, what did he manage in people, money, geography, etc.?"
- "If yours is a much smaller company, why would the candidate be attracted to you?"
- "Conversely, if the candidate is coming from a small entrepreneurial company, would she have trouble adapting to a structured corporate environment?"

Begin the Interview

Now you are ready to interview, but first you must greet your candidate. If you are picking up the candidate in the reception area and escorting him back to your office, take advantage of this brief time to relax the candidate, break the ice, and pick up some information at the same time:

- "Hi [Candidate], I'm [your name], and I'm very [eager, happy, pleased] to meet you. Did you have any trouble finding our offices?" *You might learn difficulties in commuting distance or traffic in getting to your offices.*
- *Show the candidate into your office or conference room. If you are interviewing along with another person, introduce the candidate to your associate and give the associate's title or functional description.* "[Candidate], let me introduce you to [colleague], who heads up the [name] department. [Candidate], have a seat and make yourself comfortable. Can I get you something to drink?" *It is important to relax your candidate, because a relaxed candidate will be more willing to share information with you, and that is the purpose of an interview.*
- *Begin your interview with a very brief overview of the position.* "[Candidate], we discussed the position briefly over the phone the other day, and as I said, we are looking for an individual to make a significant impact in our organization as the [title of the position]."
- *You might ask the candidate what he knows about the company.* "[Candidate], have you had a chance to read up on our company or check out our Web site?" *This may alert you as to how much preparation the candidate has done on the company, which may show interest level and initiative.*

An interview is divided up into three parts:

1. Extracting information from the candidate. *You should be talking 20 percent of the time, and the candidate should be talking 80 percent of the time. If your interview is set up for an hour, extracting information should take up the first 40–45 minutes.*

2. Sharing with the candidate the pertinent details of the position.

3. Wrapping up and determining next steps. *This is done in the last few minutes of the interview.*

Extract Valuable Information

Hiring decisions are only as good as the facts they are based on. To gather the valuable information you need, be sure to:

- Ask open-ended questions as much as possible, so the candidate has an opportunity to expand on your inquiry.
- Take detailed notes that you can refer back to when assessing your candidates.
- Work to convert each candidate's résumé (which is a marketing piece for the candidate) into a factual, chronological history of the candidate's background. Begin by establishing the candidate's present situation, and then drop back to the foundation of his education and beginning career highlights.

Phrases to extract information:

- "Tell me, are you still at the [candidate's company's name]?" *Most résumés list the most recent or current employer with a date to "present." Clarify if the candidate is still there in the event the résumé is out of date, or if he has left since he sent out the résumé.*

- "What prompts you to explore another opportunity?" *This is your first attempt to understand why he is considering leaving his company. Be prepared for a politically correct answer like, "I have gone as far as I can go, and I thought it was time to see what else is out there." Later, after you bond with the candidate, he should be more forthcoming.*

- "Let's drop back to the beginning. Tell me about your college experience." *Now we listen to the flashback storytelling of the candidate's history.*

- "Why did you choose to major in _____?" *Demonstrates early influencers and marks perhaps the first time someone has made a grown-up decision affecting future career aspirations.* "What did you hope to do in a career by majoring in that subject?" *How well did the candidate self-assess at an early age?*

- "What outside activities were you involved in?" *Demonstrates level of involvement not required and early established time-management abilities.*

- "Did you hold any elected offices?" *Demonstrates peer approval and perceived leadership skills.*

- "I see where you worked during college. How did you manage your time and still make good grades?" *Demonstrates good work ethic early on and ability to multitask.*

➡

- "Did you have any internships while in school? If so, how did you get the internship?" *Some internships are very competitive. You want to find out how many were seeking the internship, and why this candidate was chosen.*

- "How did you get your first 'real' job after graduation?" *If your candidate was offered a job through a campus recruiting program, you want to find out how competitive it was to get a job with that company.*

- "Let's talk about your first job. What did you learn the most after taking the job at [candidate's first company]?" *A person's first job has a learning component to it. It may be as structured as a six-week orientation at a training facility or on-the-job training ("Watch Bob, and do it just like Bob"). How resourceful was your candidate without the benefit of structured training?*

- "How soon were you moved into more responsibility like training others, or acting as the leader of your team, or helping in hiring new people?" *This can give you a clue as to how fast your candidate can assimilate to new concepts, become productive, and begin to offload responsibilities from a superior.*

Career Transition Question

- "What attracted you to your next job?" *This is a nice way to ask a candidate why he left a job. You may ask this question for each time a candidate leaves from one company to another to understand why. This will help gauge his tolerance level— what he will put up with, or tolerate, before he takes the step to seek another job. Without doubt, this is the most-asked question hiring managers use when assessing the right individual. Also.*

➡

- "Why did you leave that job?" *or* "Why do you want to leave your present job?"

Probe the Chronological Progression of Jobs and Experience

- "Let's talk about your other jobs." *Let the candidate "tell his story," and probe for career progression facts.*
- "At which job did you start to take on additional responsibilities?"
- "Why were you chosen to take on a more supervisory role?"
- "Why were you offered that job?"
- "Why were you promoted over your coworkers?"
- "Were you ever recruited to another company by someone you worked for in a former company? If so, explain why."
- "After the merger and layoff, why did you remain?"
- "You have been with four companies in the last two years. Can you explain why?"
- "You left the _____ industry and went into such a different industry. What prompted you to take that path?"
- "You started out in [engineering] and moved toward [marketing]. How did that happen?"
- "You quit the corporate world to start your own company. Why are you prepared to return to a more corporate job?"
- "You have several months that you were out of a job, what did you do during that time?"

As the candidate is sharing his story and revealing more about his background and career progression, eventually he

will come full circle back to his current situation. By now, there should be more of a bond between you and the candidate, where he feels comfortable talking to you and is becoming more revealing. This is the time to pinpoint his current situation, where you want to do more probing.

- "Where would you see yourself with your current company in the next year if you were to remain?"
- "What do you like most about your job, and what do you like least?"
- "You have a record for success. How will [your present employer] react to your leaving?"
- "If you were the [CEO/supervisor/manager], what changes would you make to the company or your department?"

Ensure Skill Ability

- "Let's move on to your skill level and areas of expertise." *In addition to gaining a clear understanding of the candidate's career progression, it is important to document demonstrated hard skills and credentialing to qualify skill level. Here are questions that can help accomplish this even if you do not have expertise in that area.*
  - "Explain to me the types of certification programs you have completed."
  - "Did your training or certification involve any live projects?"
  - "Was your [training/certification] delivered in a classroom, lab, or online setting?"
  - "How many people were enrolled in your training?"

➡

- "What was the instructor's background and what institution was doing the certifying? Are they recognized within the industry for credentialing? May we contact your instructor as a reference?"
- "What kind of on-the-job learning did you experience?"
- "Was there a time in any of your jobs where you were asked to train newer employees? Why do you think you were chosen?"
- "On average, how long do you think it takes to become proficient or expert in your [area of expertise]?"
- "Explain why you think you would be a quick learner of new concepts."
- "Are you required or encouraged to participate in any continuing education programs? If so, what have you participated in?"
- "How could we verify your certifications?"
- "May we contact any of your former trainers, mentors, or supervisors?"
- "May we contact any people that you helped train?"
- "What was the most challenging project you have ever been involved with, and why was it so challenging?"
- "What did you learn or take away from that project?"
- "Have you moved into a more responsible role since that experience?"

Behavioral Interviewing

Past behavior is the best predictor of future behavior, so it is essential you probe to gain perspective on a person's ability to thrive in your company, not just survive. To determine your candidate's future success probability, you should ask questions that will elicit evidence of past performance. You are not seeking what a person would do, or like to do, but rather a description of a situation she was involved with in the past, what specific action she took, and what were the final results. The answers should be detailed so there is no room for fantasy, only verifiable facts. The candidate's responses should give you information that instills confidence that she can not only perform the job willingly, but also that she can perform the job successfully. Does your candidate have not only the attitude, but also the aptitude and ability to make a significant contribution? Here are some questions that will help to ensure behavioral fit by probing a situation, learning what actions the candidate took, and determining the measurable results of that action.

Find the Right Cultural Fit

Here are questions you can use for any of a candidate's job experiences. Be sure to check your list of questions you wanted to ask when you prepared for the interview.

- "Which job position that you have had was the most rewarding and why?"
- "Which job did you like the most? Which did you like the least? Why?"
- "Tell me about a situation where you took matters into your own hands, even thought it was another person's responsibility. What was the outcome?"

- "Tell me about a time where you were asked to do really heavy business travel. How did you deal with that?"
- "Who was the most demanding [boss/job] you have ever had? How did you deal with that?" *Was the candidate resentful, or was it a learning experience?*
- "Which boss have you had that you liked the most? The least? Why?"
- "If you were the CEO, what changes would you make for the best? Do you have the opportunity to help make those changes? If not, why?"
- "Everyone from time to time has to deal with a changing environment. Tell me about a situation of change that you have gone through. How did you accept or react to the changes?"
- "Which position have you been in that had the most motivating environment? What were you able to accomplish because of that environment?"

Qualify Leadership Ability

Whether it is current management/leadership skills that are necessary for your job opening, or you are looking for future managers, here are some questions that should pull out some illustrations of their leadership aptitude and attitude.

- "Let's talk about your management style/ potential for leadership."

For more experienced managers:

- "How do you go about identifying and hiring great people for your team/company? Have you made a mis-hire, and what did you do about it?"
- "How much input do you have in the training and development of your team? How has your training improved your [processes/sales/delivery]?"

- "Describe your most challenging time in managing other people. What was the eventual outcome?"
- "How do you motivate the people that report to you? Have you had difficulty getting others to accept your ideas? What did you do about it?"
- "What is the most difficult time you have had communicating your [vision/mission] to your team?"
- "Describe a situation where you had to deal with confrontation. What was the outcome of the conflict?"
- "Tell me about an initiative that you led, the obstacles you had to overcome, and the eventual outcome."
- "How do you handle performance issues with a subordinate?"
- "Have you ever made a mistake in delegating? If so, why did you make that mistake?"
- "What is the most difficult termination you have been involved with? What were the circumstances? What was the outcome?"
- "Tell me of your most difficult decision making and how it turned out."
- "Tell me about a crisis that you encountered. How did you deal with it, and in hindsight, would you have done something differently?"
- "Describe a time where you had to turn around a morale problem with your subordinates. What eventually happened?"

For those less experienced in management or leadership:
- "What makes you think that you would be a good leader?"
  - "Tell me a time where your employer asked you to take on more responsibility as a leader. What was the result?"

- "Where have you ever had to step in and take over the lead of a project because you felt no one else was stepping up to the plate? How did you rescue the project and what were the results of your taking over?"
- "Do you like being on the idea committee or driving the details to get the job done? Describe a specific situation." *Is your candidate stronger in strategic thinking or in managing the tactical steps for execution?*
- "When have you had to organize a team together to get something done? How difficult was that for you?"
- "Did you ever hold any elected offices in school or chair any committees for a professional or nonprofit organization? What was the impact that you left on that work?" *Sometimes leadership talents are displayed more prominently in external activities than in corporate environments. Don't overlook these hidden talents.*

Qualify Team Player Attitude

Rarely does someone work in a total vacuum, so you might want to explore the dynamics of your candidate working with other team members. The ideal is a tight, cohesive team whose interactions will be synergistic to enhance productive results. A complementary group is not one where everyone thinks alike necessarily, but one where diverse thinking may promote more innovative ideas resulting in positive outcomes.

- "Let's talk about some of the people that you have worked with."
- "What was the most productive team you have ever worked on and why?"
- "Do you prefer working with a team of people or working alone? Give me examples of each."

➡

- "Have you ever seen a team fall apart because of one difficult person to deal with? How did you react to that?"
- "How competitive is it in your company between you and your peers or counterparts? Has the competitive environment helped or hurt?"
- "Have you ever been surprised at who was chosen to take the lead on a project that you were working on? Explain the situation and how it affected you."
- "Name a time when a team you worked with did not agree with you. How did you deal with that?"

Qualify Accomplishments

Encourage your candidate to toot their horn, but listen for signs of embellishment. Take notes so that you can validate what great things they are saying about themselves.

- "Let's talk about some of your successes."
- "If you were to leave your present company, how would they react? Would they panic or would they just move on? What steps do you think they would take to replace you?"
- "Tell me about your greatest professional accomplishment so far." *Or,* "What has been your proudest professional moment? What impact or legacy did you leave?"
- "Has your company recognized you for some of your accomplishments? If so, how?"
- "Have you been recognized by your industry or professional organization?"
- "Have you ever been asked to speak to a group of people? If so, explain."

- "Have you received any other awards, honors, or perks because of what you have accomplished?"
- "Have you ever received any compliments from an executive within your company?"
- "What feedback do you get normally during performance reviews?"
- "Name a time when one of your accomplishments went unnoticed. Why do you think that happened and what did you do about that?"
- "Where does your productivity rank within your company?"
- "Tell me a time where your productivity went down. Why did it happen and what did you do about it?"
- "When was the last time you received a promotion and why?"

Qualify Resiliency to Stress

Everyone has his own tolerance level to stress, which will impact how he behaves on the job. Attempt to gain information about past incidents in a candidate's work life and his reaction.

- "Everyone has to deal with work-related challenges. Let's talk about some of those."
- "What was the most difficult balancing act you have experienced in your career? How did you cope?"
- "Tell me a time when you had to juggle a heavy travel schedule with very aggressive revenue goals that your company demanded. How did you make it work?"
- "What has been the most deadline-intensive project that you have ever worked on? How did you cope with that?"

- "Have you ever felt like you were working on a project that was the 'impossible dream'? How did you deal with your superiors about it?"
- "What could you cope with least, an [out-of-touch/ micro-manager/ demanding] boss, or a coworker who is a [slacker /backstabber/ bossy]?"
- "When has your job security been threatened? What did you do about it?
- "What is the highest pressure situation you have been through in recent years? Were you able to adjust to alleviate the pressure?"

Qualify Multitasking Abilities

Many jobs require juggling multiple tasks at the same time with the ability to create a project plan and keep it on track, all of which requires finely tuned organizational skills.

- "Let's discuss your organizational abilities."
- "Are you overseeing or coordinating many projects at the same time? If so, how do you manage everything?"
- "What organizational tools do you routinely use? *For instance, Microsoft Outlook, Goldmine, Act, BlackBerry, a self-created organizational template or tool, etc.*
- "What is the greatest technology that has come along that helps you to manage all your projects and remain in communication?"
- "Walk me through a typical day where you are managing several projects at once."
- "Are you active in outside activities such as nonprofits, professional associations, church activities, volunteer positions? How does this affect your workload for your job?"

➡

- "Have you had a time in your life that you attended school while also working? Did your schoolwork suffer?"
- "What kind of system or process do you use to ensure good follow-up?"
- "Is it easy for you to refocus when jumping from one task to another? Do you feel like you are always trying to get caught up?"
- "Are you used to handling projects that are in different stages of completion? If so, what method of organization works best for you?"
- "Have you ever created or managed a project plan from beginning to end? How did you do that?"

Qualify Creative Thinking

Many positions require the ability to think outside the box. Innovative thinking is a valued commodity with the world of business and technology changing at lightning speed. An idea person who has visions of how things could be and how to make it happen can be one of your most valuable human assets.

- "Have you ever been considered the go-to person for new ideas? If so, give me an example."
- "What has been the most innovative concept you have come up with inside your company or for a client? How did your idea work out?"
- "Are you regularly asked to be involved with your company or department's strategy sessions? Why do you think that is?"
- "When you are thinking up a new way of doing things, do you visualize how it can be executed? Have you been right most of the time? Tell me a time when it didn't work out as you had planned."

- "Are you more creative with words, visual concepts, processes, or how to deal with people? Give me an example."
- "What is the most creative idea you ever came up with? What were the results?"

Qualify Initiative

Initiative is a desired trait that most employers would like to see in their employees, and in many cases, this is an innate quality that someone instinctually possesses. Occasionally a person will begin to take initiative if she feels she has been given "permission" from superiors. Here are some questions to help you discern where your candidate sits.

- "Do you feel better when you can take the bull by the horns and get the project under way? Tell me a time you did this."
- "Are you more comfortable when you have clear sailing in moving a project forward? What was the outcome of a project that you led?"
- "Tell me about how you set goals. Walk me through the planning and execution of a goal you have set."
- "Which boss gave you the most leeway in handling a project independently? Why did this happen and what were the results?"
- "What do you do when you are totally caught up at work? Do you see additional work you could do? If so, give me an example."
- "Was there ever a job that you got because you went after it?"
- "Tell me about any extra work that you have volunteered to do."

Avoid Discrimination

We live in a litigious society and it is vital that you know all the pitfalls of asking the wrong questions. As well meaning as you might be, you must be on guard to protect yourself and your company from any illegal questions that may be perceived as discriminatory. You can do a lot of study on this subject, and if you are doing a lot of hiring, that would be advised. As far as a shortcut—ask only questions that are job related. It is illegal to ask discriminatory questions regarding the candidate's gender, race, age, national origin, religion, or other non-job-related areas.

Here are questions that you can ask and those that you should avoid.

Guidelines on Interview and Employment Application Questions,
by Thomas H. Nail, SPHR, and Dale Scharinger, PhD

TOPIC	UNACCEPTABLE	ACCEPTABLE
Reliability, Attendance	–Number of children? –Who is going to babysit? –What religion are you? –Do you have pre-school age children at home? –Do you have a car?	–What hours and days can you work? –Are there specific times that you cannot work? –Do you have responsibilities other than work that will interfere with specific job requirements, such as traveling?

TOPIC	UNACCEPTABLE	ACCEPTABLE
Citizenship/ National Origin	–What is your national origin? –Where are your parents from? –What is your maiden name?	–Are you legally eligible for employment in the United States? –Have you ever worked under a different name?
Arrest and Conviction	–Have you ever been arrested?	–Have you ever been convicted of a crime? If so, when, where, and what was the disposition of the case?
Disabilities	–Do you have any job disabilities?	–Can you perform the duties of the job you are applying for?
Emergency	–What is the name and address of the relative to be notified in case of an emergency?	–What is the name and address of the person to be notified in case of an emergency? (*Request only after the individual has been employed.*)

➡

TOPIC	UNACCEPTABLE	ACCEPTABLE
Credit Record	–Do you own your own home?	–None
	–Have your wages ever been garnished?	–*Credit references may be used, if in compliance with the Fair Credit Reporting Act of 1970 and the Consumer Credit Reporting Reform Act Of 1996.*
	–Have you ever declared bank-ruptcy?	–None
Military Record	–What type of discharge did you receive?	–What type of edu-cation, training, and /or work experience did you receive while in the military?
Language	–What is your native language? Inquiry into use of how applicant acquired ability to read, write or speak a foreign language.	–Inquiry into languages appli-cant speaks and writes fluently (*if the job requires additional languages.*)

➡

TOPIC	UNACCEPTABLE	ACCEPTABLE
Organizations	–List all clubs, societies, and lodges to which you belong.	–Inquiry into applicant's membership in organizations which the applicant considers relevant to his or her ability to perform job.
Race or Color	–Complexion or color of skin.	–None
Worker's Compensation	–Have you ever filed for worker's compensation?	–None
	–Have you had any prior work injuries?	–None
Religion or Creed	–Inquiry into applicant's religious denomination, religious affiliations, church, parish, pastor, or religious holidays observed.	–None

➡

TOPIC	UNACCEPTABLE	ACCEPTABLE
Gender	–Do you wish to be addressed as Mr.?, Mrs.?, Miss?, or Ms.?	–None
Addresses	–What was your previous address?	–None
	–How long did you reside there?	–None
	–How long have you lived at your current address?	–None
	–Do you own your own home?	–None
Education	–When did you graduate from high school or college?	–Do you have a high school diploma or equivalent?
		–Do you have a university or college degree?
Personal	–What color are your eyes, hair?	–*Only permissible if there is a bona fide occupational qualification.*
	–What is your weight?	

Reprinted by permission of the Society of Human Resource Management.

Share the Right Information with the Candidate

As much as an interview should consist of 80 percent listening on the part of the interviewer, there is still that 20 percent of the interview where you are sharing vital information with the candidate about the position, the company, and expectations. After you have concluded asking the candidate open-ended questions, it is the time to reveal more information about your open position.

■ *A perfect phrase to transition into this discussion is:* "[Candidate], you have a very interesting background. I would like to tell you more about our company and the position we have open right now. Do you know much about our company?" *This answer may reveal how much research the candidate has done on your company.*

■ *Introduce your company.* "Our company is best known for [product/service/branding] and we are one of the [largest, most prestigious, fastest growing] in the [local/regional/national/global] marketplace." *Toot the company's horn regarding industry recognition, awards, or trophies.* "This is the second year we have been recognized in the industry for our outstanding contribution to the community."

■ *Explain the current situation at your company that prompts this position to be open.* "Currently, our company wants to increase our brand recognition and drive revenue on the West Coast, so we are looking for individuals who are up to the challenge of carving out a new territory for us."

➡

- *Connect the candidate's background from what you have previously heard to the current need.* "I can see how you have done a similar initiative yourself with one of your past companies, and it might very well be the type of experience we are seeking."
- *Explain the priorities of the position and a reasonable timetable.* "We expect the first six months to be very difficult and challenging, but doable with the right talent and resources."
- *Explain the rewards or type of compensation plan.* "After the first year, we would expect to achieve our [revenue number/cost containment/brand awareness], and in addition to a base salary with [bonuses/commissions/benefits] you will gain experience in _____. The salary level is open right now depending upon the candidate marketplace." *Do not quote specific salary ranges at this point, as the candidate will only hear the top end. The "marketplace" indicates that there may be competition for the candidate, and may put you in a better negotiation position later.*
- *Get a temperature check for interest.* "How does that seem to you so far?"
- *Explain the position in more depth.* "Let me tell you how we propose to start a person off in this position. First we have weeklong training and orientation at our corporate headquarters. Then we place you with another person who is doing a similar job to give you some hands-on guidance and mentoring. You will be reporting directly to [name and title], who will be discussing the company's strategy with you. On a regular basis, you will interface with [internal departments/clients/ vendors/the

➡

president's office]. There will be weekly and quarterly reporting to be done, and you would be expected to present a verbal review at any time to your superiors."

- *You must be sure to give the selling points of this job, so that when the candidate leaves and talks to his influencers (family, friends, business associates, etc.), he will have solid talking points of why this is a good opportunity to explore. You should give your candidate the perfect phrases or sound bites that can be a comeback to any influencers who are naturally skeptical.*

  - *Position the job in a compelling but realistic way.* "[Candidate], this is a position that is of high visibility and one that has a track to higher-level responsibilities and management if you are a real driver."

  - *Give an example if you can of an employee who experienced a successful career progression.* "One of our top product managers did such a great job, he has moved to a senior marketing executive position in less than two years."

  - *Give examples of perks or extras for a job well done.* "Every year we have [a holiday party/incentive trips/golf open] for people who have really excelled."

- *In the event you have a negative to overcome, such as a recent layoff reported in the press or a sagging stock market price, here are some compelling phrases. Be sure not to embellish or say what you cannot back up with facts or evidence.*

  - *Layoffs or low profitability.* "Due to some turns in the market in the last couple of years, our company had to cut back to make it operationally sustainable. We have rightsized and are back on track for a profitable picture. After careful evaluation, it seems your background and skill level could fulfill a very definite need."

- *Negative press.* "Perhaps you have seen where we have been featured in the press recently regarding a misstep in our accounting department. We have taken corrective action, and it is not something that we will tolerate again. Our company had to regroup, but we have come back stronger than ever."

End the Interview Properly

When you come to the conclusion of your interview, you should have a pretty good idea what your interest level is regarding that candidate. Either you know for sure that the candidate you have just interviewed is a definite must for further consideration, or that the candidate is absolutely not right for the job, or you just are not quite sure. You should create categories: "Yes," "Maybe," or "No." If you are interviewing a lot of people, immediately following an interview you might want to color code the candidate's résumé with Post-it notes and attach your written notes to keep track. Here are some phrases that will help you to conclude the interview with each type of candidate.

The "Yes" Candidate

You are very interested, even excited about the "yes" candidate.

- *Close in on interest level again.* "[Candidate], I really like what I hear about you and your background, does this opportunity still seem to be of interest to you?"

- *If the candidate has to give notice where she is currently working, do a reality check so you won't be surprised about a counteroffer.* "If we proceed further in a positive direction and you have to give notice, how will your employer react? Is it possible they might counter with another offer?"

- *Smoke out any concerns that the candidate may have.* "What areas of concern do you see at this point or any questions you may have?"

- *If the candidate must relocate to a new city for this position.* "What do you know about the _____ area?

➡

Do you see any obstacles standing in your way to make a smooth transition from where you are now?"

Explain Next Steps

- "Let me tell you about our interviewing process. Our next step would be for you to come in to meet with some of the others on the team." *You might want to tell the candidate about some of the others as to function and background so she can visualize others she will be working with or for.* "We have a series of interviews at this level."

- *Reference checks.* "Assuming we move forward, we will need the names of people we can contact for business references. Three to four will do, if you can gather names, titles, your relationship, and contact information, and get them back to me."

- *Application forms, background checks, and drug screens.* "In addition, we will have you fill out an application blank and sign that it is okay for us to do a background check. Be sure to be totally honest when filling out your application blank. The background check includes [driving record/criminal/credit]. There is also a drug screen that would follow."

- *Give a timeline for follow-up steps.* "You should hear from us by the end of the week regarding [scheduling for follow-up interviews/a status report on the open position/an offer]."

The "Maybe" Candidate

When the jury is out, and you are not sure if this will be a top candidate or not, assume that the candidate is a top candidate, and treat him exactly like a definite "yes" candidate. You will not have as good of an opportunity to come back and resell the position. You should, however, temper your conclusion and add a disclaimer phrase.

- "The initial interviewing process takes several [days/weeks] and we are reviewing several candidates. The selection committee will be meeting to go over résumés and deciding who will be coming back for final interviews. I will be in touch with you after that point if we proceed to the next steps with you in the interviewing process."

The "No" Candidate

You absolutely know that this person you have just interviewed is not a candidate for this position. You may have even shortened the interview knowing it was not a fit. Here are some perfect phrases to ensure that she had a good candidate experience and will leave feeling good about the company and the interview.

- "[Candidate], I want to thank you for coming in for this preliminary interview. We are interviewing a number of candidates over the next few weeks. Although you have a nice background, I am seeing résumés from candidates who have the more direct experience that we are seeking. If that changes, I will be certain to get back with you. Good luck to you on your job search."

➡

- *If there may be interest with the candidate for another position in the future.* "I want to thank you for coming in for this preliminary interview. We are interviewing a number of candidates over the next few weeks and quite frankly, I am seeing some other résumés that seem to have more direct experience in what we are seeking. However, we may have another position coming up that may be a better fit for your background. I would like to keep your résumé for that potential opening. In the meantime, good luck to you in your current job search."

Chapter 6

Conduct Due Diligence of Final Candidates

Background and reference checking will validate or nullify facts and impressions you have gathered during your interviews. If you are thorough and ask the right questions, going through this essential exercise will also bring to light new facts or experiences about a candidate. It is a way to clarify, verify, and add data to your decision making. Further, employment decisions can be legally challenged, so your best defense is to show that a reasonable and informed decision was made, including reference and background checks.

- Reference checks are interviews with people such as past supervisors, peers, subordinates, clients, and human resources professionals who can talk about your candidate's work performance and behaviors firsthand. The best person for the job of reference checking is the interviewer, as he or she is most familiar with the candidate.
- Background checks are database checks and may include criminal records, credit, litigation, department of motor vehicles, public record searches, polygraph, social security number traces, psychological, education, certifications and licenses, employment, and drug testing. Background

checks can be used to reduce the risk of theft, discipline problems, and workplace violence, and they discourage candidates from hiding information.

- In most cases, a previous employer/supervisor is able to provide job-related information about a candidate to a potential new employer. Most state laws protect that person from liability, provided the information is job related, credible, and it is without malice. Former employers will be much more inclined to provide information if there is a release signed by the candidate releasing them from liability for providing information about their previous employment.

- When you contact a reference, identify who you are, the reason for your call, and describe your open position thoroughly, as the evaluation will be more effective when it is made in relation to a specific job. Plan ahead in terms of what your questions will be and include questions that will clarify potential issues you have with a particular candidate that came up in his résumé or interview. When asking your candidates for references, try to obtain contacts that have personal knowledge of their performance and behaviors, so preferably direct supervisors and others that worked closely with the individual.

Here are some points to keep in mind when educating your hiring team to conduct effective background checks:

- Limit your reference checks to your final candidates.
- Ask your finalists' references the same overall questions for consistency. You may also want to ask a few clarifying and verifying questions that may differ from one candidate to the next based on their résumés and interviews.

- Conduct your reference and background checks prior to making a job offer and after formal interviewing, as it gives you a base of knowledge from which to gain more information.
- Always ask for work-related references, preferably supervisors.
- Contact the most recent employer, if at all possible. Unless you have been given permission, do not contact your candidate's current employer, as that may endanger his current job status. You might ask your candidate for references of employees who have left his current employer and will not endanger his standing.
- Conduct your reference checking over the telephone and take detailed notes that are factual and objective of your conversation.
- Prepare your questions in advance and get your reference to talk as long as possible. The longer a reference talks, the more forthcoming she will be about the candidate.
- If verifying education credentials, call the school registrar to verify dates and degrees, or ask the candidate to obtain sealed transcripts.
- If you receive two glowing references and one negative reference, it is best to go back to the candidate and say, "I received some information that is inconsistent with the information you provided in our interview. Can we talk about the discrepancy so you can share with me your perspective?" Listen to both sides and then make the best judgment call. You may also wish to have a second interviewer call the reference to see if there is consistency in the comments heard. If a concern of yours is raised or if you gather conflicting information, continue checking

until you are satisfied. Receiving negative feedback during the reference check does not necessarily mean that the candidate will perform poorly. Take time to allow the candidate to refute any negative comments.

■ Look for patterns of evidence and don't give undue weight to isolated incidents. Consider the possibility that the reference's comments may be based upon a particular situation.

■ If you can't get very much information from the references provided, ask your candidate for others that can provide more complete information.

■ If a reference begins talking about areas that are not job related, guide that person back to the questions at hand.

■ If a reference claims that his current employer has a policy of not providing references, call the company and confirm that this is indeed the policy. Ask the company representative if a written authorization from the candidate would suffice. If that still doesn't work, perhaps the candidate can contact former supervisors and request cooperation or perhaps there are other individuals who can be contacted. It may also be possible for the candidate to provide you with written performance appraisals from that company. If a company truly prohibits the release of information other than the verification of title and dates, always attempt to get as much information as possible. You can at least follow up with questions about the reason for separation and overall recommendation in a persistent manner.

■ To gain as much information as possible from a reference, avoid interruption.

- Only ask questions about personal characteristics if they are relevant to the position's responsibilities.
- Identify key responsibilities of the position and ask questions related to the candidate's ability and background in those areas.
- Do not ask leading questions or questions that can be answered with a simple yes or no—ask open-ended questions.
- Make sure candidates have signed a waiver granting your organization permission to contact previous employers and other references.
- Always check more than one reference.
- The Federal Fair Credit Reporting Act states that you must advise candidates of their right to know about negative information you have turned up, but only if that information is hampering their employability.
- Listen carefully to the tone of the person providing the reference and listen for silent gaps and carefully chosen words. Perhaps the reference is holding back information in these instances. When a candidate is very strong, the reference typically will be quick to answer your questions. If you hear hesitation, ask for specific examples of the candidate's work style.
- Ensure that all information you obtain is kept confidential.
- Always be consistent in everything that you do with each and every candidate!

Here are sample phrases to use when conducting a telephone reference check:

Introduction

"Hello. My name is Pamela Davis. I am a member of the recruitment committee for the position of Vice President of Marketing at ABC Brands, for which Michael Simmons is applying. Michael gave me your name as a business reference. He is being considered for employment with us. You were listed as a former employer. He has signed a release form that authorizes the release of the following information. I would like to have about 15 minutes of your time. Is this a good time to talk?" *If the reference is not available, make an appointment to call back at a more convenient time. A telephone reference call should not take longer than 20–30 minutes.*

Begin the reference check

Describe the position the candidate is applying for and include the major duties, responsibilities, and qualifications, and mention any critical skills and abilities that are being sought in candidates. "I am now going to ask you a few questions related to our open position and I would appreciate any responses you may wish to offer, which will be kept confidential. I am interested in responses based on your personal experience and interaction with Michael Simmons and behaviors that you have personally witnessed." *Avoid secondhand information, especially if it cannot be verified by the source.*

➡

Questions

Begin the questions and allow the reference ample time to respond. After you have asked your questions, ask the reference if she has any questions for you and thank the reference for taking the time to speak to you. The questions that follow are examples of questions you can ask. Many can be used or edited to fit your needs. Your questions must always be job related and never about race, religion, sex, ethnic origin, age, disability, marital status, sexual orientation, or family responsibilities.

Basic Content

- "How long have you known the candidate and in what capacity?"
- "How long did you work with the candidate?"
- "Why did the candidate leave his position?"
- "What was your professional relationship with the candidate?"
- Given the opportunity, would you rehire this candidate into the same or different job?"
- "What were the candidate's salary and bonuses at the time he left the company (if applicable)?"
- "How often did the candidate receive a salary increase?"
- "Did you promote this candidate while she worked for you?"
- "Can you verify the candidate's employment dates and most recent job responsibilities?"
- "Can you verify the candidate's reason for leaving?"

Job Content

- "What was the candidate's job title and duties?"
- "What were the candidate's main responsibilities in this job?"
- "What are the most important skills needed to succeed in this job?"
- "Can you describe a typical day for the candidate?"
- "Was the candidate frequently asked to work overtime?"
- "How did the candidate's responsibilities change or increase while he was in this job?"
- "How would you assess the candidate in comparison with others in the same job?"
- "Who did the candidate report to?"
- "Describe the common interaction required for this job."

Management Style

- "Please describe the candidate's management and leadership style."
- "How would the candidate's [managers/employees/peers/customers] describe him?"
- "How did the candidate motivate his employees?"
- "How would you characterize the relationship between the candidate and her employees and peers?"
- "What aspects of the candidate's management style were the most and least effective?"
- "How does she deal with people, especially those at lower levels?"
- "How would you describe the candidate's leadership skills, and are you aware of any conflicts with staff?"

Performance

- "How would you describe this candidate's overall job performance?"
- "How would you describe this candidate's work style?"
- "What are the candidate's greatest strengths?"
- "How did this candidate compare with others in your department who were performing the same job?"
- "Describe this candidate's work quality and give me an example."
- "What would have made the candidate even more effective in her job?"
- "Did the candidate meet or exceed your expectations?"
- "The candidate is being considered for a position as a _____. Do you feel that the candidate is capable of being successful in this type of job?"
- "On a scale of 1 to 10 (10 is excellent and 1 is poor), how well did he perform?"
- "In your opinion, in what area does he require more training and development?"
- "How would you describe the quality and/or quantity of the candidate's work?"
- "How did the candidate respond to criticism and what was her ability in resolving interpersonal conflicts?"
- "Did you ever have to discipline the candidate for misconduct or violation of company policies?"
- "Would you recommend this person for the position he has applied for?"
- "Was the candidate's work performed satisfactorily?"
- "Did the candidate earn promotions?"
- "What did the candidate accomplish that made a significant difference to your organization?"

➡

- "Did you ever have to talk to the candidate about performance problems? What were the issues?"
- "How did the candidate learn the job? Do you recommend any training methods?"
- "What support will the candidate need to perform well on the job?"
- "This position requires _____. How would you describe the candidate's ability to perform these requirements?"

Skills and Abilities

- "How would you compare the candidate's skills with others performing in the same job?"
- "How would you rate the candidate's leadership skills? Why?"
- "Is the candidate more suited to a strategic role or one that is more tactical?"
- "Is the candidate stronger in her analytical abilities or her execution abilities?"
- "How would you evaluate the candidate's communication skills? Can you give me some examples? Have you seen her written work or heard the candidate speak?"
- "Please describe the candidate's ability in the area of _____. Can you give me a specific example?"
- "How would you describe the candidate's work habits, especially in his ability to initiate, implement, and follow through on projects? Do you have an example?"
- "What else would you like to add that would assist us in evaluating the candidate's qualifications?"
- "How would you describe the candidate's organizational skills?"
- "How would you rate the candidate's ability to think creatively?"
- "How would you describe the candidate's interpersonal skills?"
- "Can you give me some examples that demonstrate the candidate's technical abilities?"
- "Can the candidate multitask and consistently meet deadlines?"
- "How would you rate the candidate's ability to plan short-term and long-term?"

- "How would you describe the candidate's decision-making ability and timeliness?"
- "How would you describe the candidate's ability to build effective working relationships with peers? Is the candidate a team player?"

Personal Traits

- "How would you rate the candidate's ability to pay attention to detail?"
- "How would you rate the candidate's ability to learn new skills and follow directions?"
- "How much supervision did the candidate require?"
- "How does the candidate react to and work under pressure?"
- "How would you describe the candidate's general overall attitude toward his work?"
- "How would you describe the candidate's ability to work independently and act on her own initiative?"
- "Is the candidate reliable and dependable, and does she follow through?"
- "The candidate comes across as [outgoing, personable, aggressive]. Is what you see basically what you get?"
- "Is the candidate flexible and able to effectively handle change? Does change frustrate this candidate? Can you give me an example?"
- "Did the candidate consistently support your company rules and ethics?"
- "Was the candidate reliable?"
- "Did the candidate get along with coworkers, supervisors, and customers?"
- "Was this candidate a team player?"
- "Was this candidate motivated and a self-starter?"
- "Did the candidate exhibit honesty and integrity?"
- "How well did the candidate manage crisis, pressure, and stress?"

Other

- "What would be an ideal position for this candidate?"
- "What is your advice to best motivate this candidate?"
- "What would you do differently if this candidate worked for you again?"
- "What is the best way to develop this candidate and his/her skills?"
- "How long have you known the candidate and in what context?"
- "What does she really care about and what motivates her?"
- "What would his critics say about him?"
- "What haven't I asked you that you might be able to give insight into that would help me to better evaluate her?"
- "Is there anything I haven't asked you that might be important to know about his ability to succeed in this position?"
- "Who else do you know that may be able to give me some good insights into this candidate?"
- "Is there anything else you would like to add regarding the candidate's job performance?"
- "Has the candidate ever been disciplined or investigated for misconduct?"
- "Are you able to enthusiastically recommend this candidate?"
- "What were the circumstances and reason for this candidate's separation from your company?"
- "Can you provide dates of employment?"
- "How would you describe the candidate's relationships with coworkers, superiors, and subordinates?"
- "Could you compare the candidate to the person doing the job now?"

➡

- "What are you going to look for in the candidate's replacement?"
- "No one is perfect in everything. Please describe some of the candidate's shortcomings."
- "I'd like to read you the description of the candidate's job with your organization from his résumé. What comments do you have?"
- "Did the candidate have a positive or negative work attitude? Please elaborate."
- "What is your overall assessment of the candidate?"
- "Would you recommend her for this position? Why or why not?"
- "Is the candidate eligible for rehire? Why or why not?"
- "What was the reason given for leaving your organization?"
- "Is there anything of significance that you would like to add?"
- "What was the candidate's beginning and ending salary (if applicable)?"

Conducting due diligence on your final candidates should always be part of your hiring practices, but remember that background and reference checks are not always foolproof. They are simply tools to help you make an informed decision and help to avoid negligent hiring. The information you may obtain will also be helpful to provide to your new hire's supervisor for performance development and insights into this person's strengths and weaknesses.

Use your own judgment and don't allow your checks to be a substitution for your decision making. Make sure your decisions are based on *all* of the facts you have collected throughout the hiring process.

Chapter 7

Manage Candidates and Their Interest Effectively

Do a Temperature Check with Your Candidate

When closing an interview with a candidate, it is important to check his interest level and determine any concerns he may have. You want to make sure that you have the opportunity to give him the right information to offset his concerns if possible. There are many perfect phrases that can help you accomplish this:

- "Now that we have discussed in more detail the nature of this position, what is your interest level?"
- "Can you visualize yourself in this role?"
- "What questions do you have about the job position?"
- "What concerns do you have in considering this position?"
- "What do you think would be your greatest challenge in taking this position?"
- "Do you see any barriers that would prevent you from taking this position?"
- "What sounds the most interesting to you about this job?"
- "Why would you be the right person for this position?"
- "This position sounds very similar to what you have done before. Why would this position be more attractive to you?"
- "Would you be interested in meeting some of our people who are presently doing this job?"
- "All things being equal in compensation, is this the right position for you?"

The WOW Factor

Many interviewers fall into the trap of thinking that everyone should clamor to work for their company, so it is the candidate who needs to sell the employer that she is the person for the job. This is only partly true, as the selection process is a two-way street, and even more so now and in the coming years as we face a shortage of skilled candidates. A candidate does not live in a vacuum or stay on a shelf in between interviews or communications. You can rest assured that even a passive candidate who wasn't looking when you found her will begin to look around to see what else is out there. It only makes sense that if a passive candidate has chosen to explore an opportunity with your company, she will want to investigate others. After all, if she is going to make a decision to leave her present position, she wants to make sure it is for the best opportunity out there. It is vital that you impress your top candidates with why people like working at your company. Begin by thinking why you like working there, and poll others for their reasons. Nothing is too small for consideration when it comes to your selling points for working for your company.

- "Did I mention that in addition to our normal benefits we have [free parking/annual company picnic/President's Club trip/flextime]?"
- "Last year our company was recognized as number one in customer service, which we have won for the past three years."
- "We have a very good career path with our company. The reason this position is open is that we promoted that person to a higher management position."

- "Our company experiences very little turnover, which is probably due to [list some of the reasons your employees like working for your company]."
- "The leadership of our company is really stellar, our CEO came from _____ and has accomplished _____."
- "We just came out with a new product that is way ahead of the competition, and it is crushing their marketshare."
- "We take pride in hiring only the best." *Your candidate will want to be included in this group.*

Maintain Continuity and Communication with Your Top Candidates

There is nothing more disconcerting to a candidate than to not know where he stands in the selection process. The longer the time that passes between interviews or communications, the more opportunity the candidate has to stray or reconsider his interest. During the interview and selection process, it is vital that a person is appointed to be the "shepherd" for that candidate. This can be someone from Human Resources or a hiring manager, but it's important that someone is in charge of the candidate; otherwise, you run the risk of going through the entire time-consuming selection process only to lose an outstanding candidate to a competing opportunity or through self-elimination.

The shepherd should debrief with the candidate after each interview that is conducted with other hiring managers in the selection process. It is vital to know if there is any change in the air.

- ▪ "How did your interview with _____ go?"
- ▪ "After meeting with _____, is he someone you think you would like working [with/for]?"
- ▪ "Did _____ elaborate in more detail the nature of the position? How do you feel about his perspective?"
- ▪ *If there is going to be a lapse in time until another interview or a decision, set expectations with your candidate.*
  "[Candidate], the next person you will be meeting in the interview process is out of town until late next week. We probably won't be able to schedule your meeting until he gets back. Will that time delay work within your job search timeline?"

Prepare Your Candidate for External Influencers

A candidate rarely makes a job change decision without consulting with his network of friends, colleagues, and family. All of these external influencers play a part in the candidate's decision about whether the job is for him. In fact, most candidates are on their cell phone before they leave the parking lot to talk to someone close to them to tell them how the interview went. As the interviewer or hiring manager, you must give your candidate the "talking points" for subsequent conversations with outside influencers.

■ *As a hiring employer, you may never have the opportunity to talk to your candidate's influencers, but you must consider that there might be a devil's advocate in the mix, or a person who has a negative opinion about your candidate leaving her present position.* "Is there anyone in your sphere of influence that would say that this is not the right job for you?"

■ *Give your candidate company literature or handouts.* "[Candidate], here is some literature about our company that might be helpful in explaining all about our divisions and locations around the world. Also, here is a brochure explaining our medical benefits, which are considered very generous." *A spouse or other influencers need tangible evidence that will impress them with the stature of your company. Company literature should speak for you as to the benefits of working for your company.*

■ *If you are a start-up company, you must sell a convincing vision of where you are going in order to compete with*

more established companies. "We are a new company, but our founders have a recognized background of accomplishments that spell success. I see this as a ground-floor opportunity for the person who would love to start and create from a clean slate."

- *If your company has suffered from unflattering press, or you are involved with a turnaround situation, again, you must paint a picture of what early success looks like.* "Our stock has been in the doldrums for the past year, but we have a plan in place that is beginning to show a turn in our business. Our goals are very reachable, and we are on schedule. The way we are going, the next five years look very rosy. We are looking now for our future leaders to take us into the next level."

Detect any Relocation Obstacles

Many people resist change, and this can be quite evident in a candidate's family, especially if there is a relocation involved. Relocation decisions are usually family based, and relocation is a foremost consideration in taking a new position. The candidate's spouse may have a career in her present city that may be difficult to transfer to another city, or the candidate's children may be reluctant to move from their friends at school. It could be that your candidate is going through a divorce, and his spouse may not even know that he is contemplating a job in another city. You must be careful here because you may not legally inquire about a candidate's spouse or children. After an offer is made, you may inquire, as the offer was not contemplated based upon family considerations.

- "Are there any challenges you would face in a relocation to our city?"
- "Have you been a visitor to our city before? I would be glad to get you information about our city, the housing market, schools, places of worship, and shopping." *If your company does not have this information handy, you should connect with your local chamber of commerce to see what literature they may have that you can send out to your out-of-town candidates. You can also refer your candidates to Web sites that can give information that is sponsored by the local chambers. You may also want to connect with a real estate brokerage to handle relocation of new employees. Most real estate brokerages have welcoming packages for relocating families.*

- *The more remote your job location is, the more information your candidate will need. Investing the time in compiling points of interest in your locale can really pay off in recruiting and attracting the right person. Remember what won't work for one person may be just the object of attraction to another.* "Our town is several miles from [the closest major city], but many people love it here because it is a great place to raise a family and really become part of a community. There are no traffic problems, and land is inexpensive compared to the big cities. If you like the outdoors, there is a lot of fishing, hunting, and hiking that people here seem to enjoy."

After the offer is made and before acceptance, you may ask more pertinent questions to aid in relocation. Most candidates considering an offer will want to come to your city with their spouse to look at the housing market, and to see what neighborhoods would be the right place for them. If you don't have a relocation department, team up with a real estate brokerage. In expectation of selling a home to your new employees, a brokerage can do a lot of work for you. Here are some phrases for discussing relocation:

- "What is the housing market like where you live now?"
- "Do you have any unusual moving requirements?" *You might have a candidate who lives on a farm and wants to move ten head of cattle. You want to be prepared for unusual requests and potential associated costs.*
- "Would your family want to move before the school year is out or on break, or would they prefer to wait until then?" *Many relocating families don't want to interrupt the*

➡

school year, so a spouse and the children might remain behind until the school has a break and while their current home is on the market. You might need to provide temporary housing until that time for your candidate.

- "Since your youngest child has two more years in high school, would that present a problem regarding moving?" *This can be an issue, as the parents will be empty nesters in two years when a move may be much more convenient, and they will not have to move their high school–aged child to another school in the midst of determining what college they might attend.*

- "Does your spouse have a career that is easily transferable? Perhaps I can refer your spouse to an executive search company that specializes in that area." *During the interviewing process when you have to call your candidate to make travel arrangements, call him at home and announce who you are and give your candidate a travel itinerary. If the spouse answers, listen to her tone of voice and see if there is enthusiasm or the opposite in her voice. This might give you a clue as to any resistance your candidate might be experiencing within the family.*

Confront Potential Counteroffers

Great talent is in short supply, and companies are pulling out all stops to retain the good employees they already have. If you have identified what you consider a top talent who is presently employed, you can assume the candidate's employer will not want to lose that person just as much as you would like to hire that person. You should prepare early on in the hiring process to confront the possibility of a counteroffer to the candidate you have fallen in love with.

- "How will your company react when you decide to leave?" *You want your candidate to begin to visualize the reality of leaving.*

- "How will your boss react to your giving notice?" *Notate body language, as giving verbal notice is usually a very difficult step to take whether you love or hate your boss.*

- "How would you react if your company made a counteroffer to you?" *The candidate's response may give you information about his employer's policy on counteroffers. Some companies may have a policy to never make a counteroffer.*

- "What if your company made an offer for [more money/less travel] ?" *You want to determine what the candidate would do if the reason he is looking is reversed. You in turn might respond:* "Wouldn't you be suspect if it took giving notice for your company to recognize that you were being underpaid? Is the real root of why you are looking still going to be there?"

- "How would your company replace you?" *You would like to find out if there is a succession plan in place at your*

candidate's employment, because if not, a company will many times counter with the VIP treatment. In an effort to keep a great employee, especially when not easily replaced, unusual reactions may happen, like golfing with the CEO, a move to the corner office, or even a country club membership.

- "Research shows that nine out of ten people who accept a counteroffer leave within the year anyway." *When a person accepts a counteroffer, the original trust is compromised. An employer will move into Plan B to make sure they are not ever caught off guard again and that there is a replacement in the wings. That new team member may begin to shadow the person who has accepted the counteroffer to better step into the role if need be. The person begins to see signs of being out of the loop or his opinion is no longer sought. The shift of importance may be subtle at first, but soon snowballs once the VIP glow wears off, and the underlying issues that were there in the first place still remain.*

- "I know you are in the middle of your job search. Do you have other opportunities that you are seriously considering?"

- "How does this opportunity compare to others you are exploring?"

- "Taking salary out of the equation, which position seems to be the best fit for you?" *Salary considerations are always paramount, but if the job is not the real pull for the candidate, it might not be the right fit for you or the candidate.*

- "Where are you in the interviewing process with your other opportunities?" *Candidates who have decided to*

➡

explore other opportunities may not want to accept the first offer if others are anticipated. If yours is the first offer, you may have to wait for the outcome of the other competing companies. If you are willing to wait, get a time frame commitment from your candidate.

Pre-Close Your Candidate During the Interview Process

You should be closing your candidate from the very first interview, with each succeeding meeting more conclusive about the seriousness of his interest in your opportunity. Here are some perfect phrases to pre-close in graduating intensity.

- "Does this position seem to be a good move for you? How?"
- "Is this the right career step for you in your life right now?"
- "Does this job seem to have your name on it?"
- "Now that I have described the position, does this still seem interesting to you?"
- "Now that I have described the position, can you visualize yourself in this role?"
- "What do you like the most about this position?"
- "Do you see this as a challenging position for you at this stage of your career? How?"
- "If you could create your own position, is this the one for you?"
- "You have done such a great job for your present company, why would you really want to leave?"
- "Other than salary, what other benefits or perks do you particularly value?"
- "If we were to make you an offer, what would be your availability to start?"
- "What would prevent you from taking this job?"
- "I am pretty sure we will have an offer coming down the pike. Is this the job offer you would feel comfortable in accepting?"
- "What kind of notice do you need to give to your company?"

Part Three

Hiring and Transitioning Top People Into Your Organization

Chapter 8

Negotiate an Offer Without Any Hitches

Is It All About the Money?

There are many reasons a person accepts a new job position. One of the top considerations is the compensation that is being offered, but it is by no means the only thing. Other considerations could be medical benefits, vacation policy, tuition reimbursement, travel considerations, training and learning opportunities, the reputation of the company, and advancement opportunities, amongst others. Basically, there are two types of considerations that a candidate takes into account when making a decision to accept or decline an offer: (1) those that have a hard dollar value like base salary, and (2) those that have an emotional value such as advancement potential.

It is important to know what you have to offer, what the perceived value is to your candidate, and how to quantify that value into your offer negotiations. In an ideal world, an offer should be an upward move for the candidate monetarily, psychologically, and emotionally. Monetarily, a typical upward move can be between 5 to 20 percent of the candidate's present monetary compensation. That means all of the hard dollar valuations that are paid to a candidate should be considered in your calculations for an offer.

First, it is vital to know what your candidate's total compensation package has been at her most recent job to better understand how to position your offer. You have probably asked on the front end when you were telephone screening your candidates, but you may not have many details other than total compensation. This can be a delicate dance, as your candidate has very likely been coached not to say anything about her present compensation plan first, for fear of losing her leverage. It is best to know as much as possible to formulate an offer that is attractive to your candidate and is within the budget you have set for this new person. Here are some phrases to extract the information you need:

- "[Candidate], would you describe your current compensation plan?" *This is pretty straightforward, but you want to make sure the candidate includes all hard dollar elements, such as:*
  - *Base salary*
  - *Variable compensation (bonuses, commissions, other comp based upon performance)*
  - *Medical and health-care benefits*
  - *Retirement, pension, or savings plan*
  - *Vacation or personal time off*
  - *Incentive trips or contests with monetary value*
  - *Operational expenses such as car, gasoline, cell phone, laptop allowance*
  - *Tuition reimbursement*
  - *Flextime or telecommuting*
- *If your candidate is reticent on giving compensation information, you should say this:* "If we move into an offer situation, I really need to know a complete

compensation description so that we can better formulate an appropriate offer for you."

- "How long have you had your current base salary?" *Or,* "When was your last raise?" *You want to know when the candidate has received the last raise on his base salary to indicate if he is expecting a raise in the near future. Or if a recent raise has taken place, has the candidate become used to the increase in salary?*

- "Explain how your variable compensation works." *Is the variable compensation based specifically upon the candidate's performance, such as a sales commission based upon a commission formula? Or is the variable compensation based upon a combination of personal performance and the overall performance or profitability of the company? If the latter, you must make a determination of the company's viability to pay out bonuses based upon company performance. If times are tough for that company or industry, you may gain a negotiation chip here.*

- "Has your company paid out bonuses every year?" *Just because a bonus plan is in place does not mean that bonuses are paid out. If the company has not paid out bonuses in past years, this may be another negotiation chip.*

- "How is your bonus calculated?" *Many bonuses are calculated on a certain percentage spread of an annual base salary. Find out what the spread is, and what the percentage history has been in the last few years.*

- "Of all the people in your position at your company, how many received bonuses or commissions?" *If in sales,* "What was your ranking compared to other salespeople with your company?" *You want to get a comparison between your candidate and others that are counterparts to see how he stacked up against his coworkers. If your candidate is of top ranking, this may give you an idea on what you may have to do in the way of compensation to attract him to your company.*

■ "What are your current medical and health care benefits, and does your company pay any portion of your medical benefits?" *The costs of health care benefits has been on a steady rise, and has a concrete dollar impact on a person's earnings, not to mention medical benefit plans are as diverse as there are companies. Find out what premium costs, if applicable, the company absorbs, and what out-of-pocket the candidate pays, so you can compare that to what you have to offer. See if the health care benefits cover any other dependent coverage, which can be of particular importance to someone who has a dependent with an ongoing illness. You can't ask that question, but if you move into an offer scenario, this importance may come out. Health care benefits may include dental, vision, long-term or short-term disability, among other benefits, such as long-term care, cancer insurance, or life insurance.*

■ "Does your company have a 401(k) or other retirement plan where there are matching dollars?" *Many employers have savings programs where they will match a certain percentage or dollar amount that the employee puts into a retirement account. You want to see if your candidate has taken advantage of this type of plan, as this may be a hard dollar value that the employee views as a benefit. A 401(k) plan is completely portable and may be taken with the employee at any time he leaves his employment.*

■ "Are you fully vested in your retirement plan at present, or how long before you would be fully vested?" *Most employers have an employment duration that must be met before the employee is completely eligible for a pension or other type of retirement plan outside of a 401(k). If your candidate has met the time requirements, the pension becomes fully vested, but if not, or if she is close to fulfilling her vesting period, your candidate might be inclined to stay where she is until that date, unless an offer would offset the lost dollar value.*

- "How much vacation time or personal time off do you currently have?" *There is real dollar value here, and some people may have worked up to a three- or four-week vacation if not more. If your company has a policy of the typical two weeks' vacation until employed over a certain number of years, you will have a problem convincing a candidate to ignore the additional vacation he has enjoyed. You may need to reconsider revamping your vacation policy to be commensurate with a candidate's vacation benefits, especially if you are seeking people with multiple years work experience. Personal time off, holidays, and sick days should also go into the equation when calculating your offer.*

- "Have you ever participated in any incentive trips or company contests?" *Winning a trip or other type of contest has monetary value and the IRS demands that the value needs to be declared as part of income. Winning a contest and the recognition that goes along with that also has emotional value that may have an impact on a candidate making a decision on an offer, especially if that contest involved the candidate's family.*

- "Does your company cover expenses for a car, gasoline, cell phone, or laptops?" *These operational expenses can really add up when a candidate calculates monthly expenses, especially if he is used to any of these items being paid for by his company. The covered expenses may offset a car payment, gas expenses, and cell phone use that is normal everyday usage even for personal use. Again, these items need to be part of your calculation for an offer.*

■ "Does your company offer tuition reimbursement or is that something you have contemplated?" *If your candidate is already enrolled into a tuition reimbursement program, you can bet that this is an important consideration until after graduation, as tuition for higher education can be very expensive.* "Does your company have any requirements that must be met to qualify for tuition reimbursement?" *Most employers have a grade threshold that must be met in order to receive tuition reimbursement benefits. Tuition reimbursement benefits can be a huge dollar value, depending on the school and advanced degree program.*

■ "Does your employer offer flexible hours or telecommuting? *To some candidates, flexible work hours or the ability to telecommute can trump a lesser base salary if a long commute appears unattractive.*

Determine Who Your Competition Is

In a tight employment market, it is essential to clearly understand who your competition is. Even if you have convinced a passive candidate to explore an opportunity with your company, assume that at some time during the interview process your candidate will kick the tires of other companies. After all, if a person is going to leave her present company for another opportunity, it makes sense she moves to the best opportunity. Just like you are doing your due diligence in hiring the best candidate, the candidate should do her own due diligence in making the decision to move.

This can be an awkward exchange with your candidate, somewhat like asking someone if he is dating anyone else he likes better. Here are some phrases that can help you through this delicate but important fact-finding mission.

- "What stage of your job search are you in?"
- "It is a very different job market compared to a few years ago. How do you find it?"
- "How does this opportunity compare to others you are exploring?"
- "What seems to be the most important aspect of this opportunity compared to others?"
- "Do you have any other outstanding job offers you are considering?"
- "If you take money out of the equation, does this sound like the perfect job for you? How?"
- "Does this opportunity have more career advancement potential than others you are looking at?"
- "Would it make sense to do a pro/con exercise on this and the other opportunity you are looking at?"

➡

- "In weighing this and other opportunities, what information can I get for you that will aid in your decision-making process?"
- "What would prevent you from accepting our offer?"

Making the Offer

If you have come this far in your selection process and are ready to make an offer, you are almost home free, but don't assume anything is complete until there is an offer, an acceptance, an agreement on compensation, and a start date. You are entering the offer process, and eleventh-hour issues may crop up. Here are phrases that can help avoid a last-minute misunderstanding.

- "We are formulating an offer for you and will be getting an offer letter out to you. Assuming everything is as expected, when can we expect for you to start?"
- "Congratulations, [Candidate]! I am excited about making an offer to you for the position of [title of position]. The offer is [total comp value], to include [base salary amount/bonus percentage/ commission plan/ vacation /personal time off]. In addition, there is a [401(k) plan/pension plan/profit sharing plan] and a health-care plan where we absorb [premium cost amount] for you. There is dependent coverage if you would like, and I would be happy for you to talk to our benefits administrator to discuss dependent coverage." *Negotiations may step up a notch if your candidate has medical issues with anyone in his family. Be prepared for your candidate to take time with your benefits administrator or study the health-care benefits manual in depth. There can be real out-of-pocket expenses for this type of candidate, and the health-care benefit plan may be a deal breaker.* "Other benefit offerings are [car allowance/cell phone/laptop/ tuition reimbursement/company sales contest/flex hours]."

➡

- "We will be sending out an offer letter outlining what I have already mentioned. When can we expect to hear back from you regarding our offer? Do you see any immediate concerns?" *Every 24 hours that passes after an offer is made without an acceptance reduces your chances of a successful close. You should give your candidate a time limit.* "Generally we would like to hear back from candidates regarding our offer [within two business days/over the weekend]."
- "Can I help in getting any more information to you so you can come to a decision that is right for you?"
- "How will accepting this position at this time affect your career or your family?" *Since you have made an offer, there is nothing to prevent you from inquiring how this new position will impact others, including family members. This is not perceived as potential discrimination, as you have already made the offer, but should help the candidate in coming to the proper decision on whether this is the right job for her.*

Counter the Counteroffer

We have already discussed in Chapter 7 the importance of the counteroffer coming from the candidate's present employer. This is definitely part of assessing the competition, and may be the most common type of competition to be considered. Making a career move from one situation to another means going from a known environment to an unknown environment. Some people can be very intimidated by change, and even though the issues at a candidate's present company are very real, compelling the candidate to seek an outside opportunity, it is still familiar territory. You must be prepared if your candidate elects to remain where he is, or if while attempting to resign he accepts a counteroffer from his present employer.

Chapter 9

Make Your New Employees Feel at Home

Your star candidate has just accepted your job offer with enthusiasm and gratitude. You both have agreed on a start date and you can't wait to have your new employee on your team. With the taxing hiring process now behind you, it's time to relax, right? Absolutely not! A critical driver of profitability is accelerating the time a new employee takes to get up to speed. After the hiring and selection process, this is the single most critical step to ensure the early success of your new employee. It is accomplished by implementing a properly structured "on-boarding" process beginning right after your candidate says yes and lasting for at least three to six months after the initial start date. Extending a sound on-boarding process to at least three to six months is now more vital than ever, as employee turnover is consistently rising.

On-boarding is the process of fully integrating and not just orienting new employees into their new work environment to accelerate their impact. It's much more than just an orientation to Human Resources policies and procedures. Implementing a rapid on-boarding program allows new employees to learn the ropes effectively with fewer obstacles getting in their way during the initial days, weeks, and months they are on the job, and, therefore, they will generate value much more quickly.

Every action and every communication has consequences, sharing with the new employee something about your organization. A poorly organized orientation says something very different about an organization than a highly engaging, organized, and professional program. If your company demands high levels of performance and attention to detail of every employee, then your organization must show this same commitment to employees, especially early on. Showing your company cares is one of the strongest drivers of employee engagement. You want your new employees to feel as though they have joined a world-class outfit.

New employees do not want to be perceived as needy or high maintenance. They try not to complain or voice their concerns. This is why you need to make it comfortable for new hires to give you consistent and honest feedback. Conduct entrance interviews rather than wait for exit interviews to find out what's wrong. The most vulnerable time frame for new hires is usually during the first six-month period. Here are some questions you can ask your new employees during an entrance interview and then at two- to four- week intervals after that:

- "How is your job and how is everything going?"
- "Is it what you expected when you were hired? If no, why not?"
- "Have you come across any surprises? If yes, what are they?"
- "How was the new employee orientation? How would you improve it?"
- "How is your relationship with your new manager and colleagues?"
- "Do you have all the tools you need to do your job?"

- "Have you visited the company's intranet site? Is it easy to navigate?"
- "Is there anything else that you need that you don't yet have access to?"
- "How would you compare what we said we would be like during the recruiting phase versus what we are really like?"
- "What is going really well?"
- "Which employees have been exceptionally helpful to you?"

These questions address issues that can affect morale and performance, and the answers can provide your company with valuable information to continually improve your on-boarding experience.

You never get a second chance to make a first impression, so your company should make sure your new hire feels welcomed, comfortable, valued, and prepared for what lies ahead. Begin this process by first establishing the goals of the on-boarding program and the specific, measurable results you want to accomplish during this period.

1. Step One: Ask yourself, "At the end of this program, after [period of time], the employee will be _____." Include all critical success factors you may have previously established for the job description.
2. Step Two: Develop a specific on-boarding calendar to lay out all related action items for day one, week one, month one, month two, etc. Also, be sure to get consistent feedback from your new employee to determine what is working and what is not.
3. Step Three: Remember that a key to success is joint accountability between the new hire and the new hire's manager for the new hire's development. The manager

should also be responsible for the completion of the development and on-boarding plan. It is also important to note that there are on-boarding software solutions that can assist with providing easy access to administrative and Human Resources–related items such as payroll, health benefits, etc.

The following sections provide checklists of on-boarding activities that you can provide to all of your line managers and executives to ensure your employees' success at every level. These checklists of items should be monitored and measured. The duration of the program can be up to six months or longer depending on your goals. Generally, the goals of the first 90 days are to make sure the new employees truly believe they made the right decision to join your organization and to make them productive team players as quickly and efficiently as possible. It takes a multitude of coordinated acts to accomplish a successful employee integration.

Pre–First Day Checklist

- The days between the offer letter and the first day of work should consist of information flow between your new hire and the company to make sure your employee remains excited about his opportunity and he isn't tempted by other offers or opportunities. Has your new employee filled out forms during this period to save time on the first day? Forms to consider include standards of conduct, W-2s, direct deposits, ordering business cards, etc.

- Have you provided communications that reinforce the company's brand, such as news articles, annual reports, and employee handbooks?

- Have you provided detailed directions for getting into the office, especially if there are security measures?

- Have you provided orientation materials online so new employees can view this information prior to starting in their new role? Include information such as benefits forms, background company information, and orientation meeting schedules and procedures. When your new employee goes home to report his first day to his family, it would be better to have him talk about something he's excited about rather than the fact that he filled out lots of forms. Have you created an online center where new employees can find materials, information, and forms as they need them and as they settle into their new role?

- A new hire will become instantly frustrated and be unproductive if she cannot immediately access building facilities, computer systems, e-mail, and telephone messaging. Have you completed paperwork and processes well in advance so these areas are working on day one?

➡

- Little things mean a lot. Prior to day one, have you ensured some of these things are available on the first day—business cards, office space and supplies, secretarial support, systems access, staff directories, paycheck information, and building maps?
- Have you managed expectations during the recruiting process and accurately shaped the candidate's expectations, even from the first conversations about the opportunity? Promises should not be conveyed unless they can be delivered, especially in the areas of reporting structure, promotional opportunities, responsibilities, pay, and organizational plans.
- Have you made sure the spouse or family feels welcomed into your company's family? Sometimes a simple gesture such as a handwritten note can do wonders.
- Have you sent a welcome letter, directions to enter the building and department, parking information, schedule for the first week, and any other information about the job and department?
- Has your staff been informed of the new employee— name, title, start date, responsibilities?
- Has an office or workspace been prepared with all necessary supplies, including a name plate?
- Have office keys and badges been ordered?
- Has a mentor been assigned to help acclimate the new employee?
- Has the mailroom been notified to add the new employee to the mailing list?
- Have you evaluated what introductory information your new hire needs and made it available before he reports to work?

➡

- Have you introduced your new hire to other key employees who can "champion" her cause—even before the official start date—and invited your new hire to contact any of these employees to ask questions?
- Have you invited your new hire to key meetings, even prior to the start date?

First Day (Orientation) Checklist

Don't make this day all about paperwork. This first day will have an impact on your new employees, so make it a welcoming and effective experience.

- Have you provided business cards, tools such as phones and computers, benefits information, office space and supplies, software, a phone directory, organization charts, user IDs and e-mail accounts, and name plates?
- Have you cleared your calendar so that you can physically be there on day one? The supervisor is the ideal person to introduce the new employee around.
- Have you sent an announcement communication regarding your new employee, describing his expertise, responsibilities, and interests to others?
- Have you signed up your new employee for mailing and distribution lists and online groups she'll need to be part of?
- Have you provided detailed job expectations and measures for the first 90 days in a written performance agreement and a copy of the job description?
- Have you greeted your employee on his first day and taken him to lunch, or have you arranged for someone else to take on this task if you as the hiring manager are unavailable?
- Have you persuaded your new employee to ask questions and to network?
- Have you performed a standard orientation on company, culture and mission, team orientation, and values?
- Have you set aside time so that the new employee can sit with you or her new hiring manager to ask questions?

- Have you designated a "mentor" who is responsible and accountable and can assist with making introductions during the first few weeks? Have you arranged for the mentor and the new employee to meet on a regular basis?
- Have you incorporated a training program depending on the nature of the position and the qualifications of the new employee?
- If your orientation is all about rules and red tape, don't neglect components that communicate the following messages to new employees: "We're excited to have you onboard," "You are now part of a truly wonderful organization," and "This is why your job is so important." Have you ensured that these three human needs (and motivators) are addressed from the very beginning—the need for meaning and purpose, the desire to matter, and the desire for esteem?
- Have you scheduled senior-level executives to talk with new hires so they can understand the big picture and the important role they will play in contributing to the overall goals of the company?
- Have you placed a simple welcome packet on the new employee's desk that includes a company cup or pen or anything else that shows that he has been welcomed to the team?
- Have you sent your new employee a welcoming voice mail or e-mail?
- Have you created a comfortable environment by implementing the following strategies?
  - Give a warm welcome and discuss the plan for the first day.

➡

- Tour the assigned workspace and locations for rest rooms, refreshments, and immediate areas, and provide required keys and badges.
- Arrange to have lunch with the employee.
- Introduce employee to staff members and a mentoring buddy.
- Review the nature and responsibilities of the job, organization chart, and department.
- Review policies and procedures, including working hours, telephone, e-mail, and Internet use, office supplies organization, office resources (manuals, directories, etc.), staff meetings, accountability, confidentiality, ethics, and customer service.

- Have you provided an overview of the department's function and organization chart and explained the relationship of the department to other departments?
- Have you met with the employee at the end of the day to answer any questions about the first day?
- If your new employee is a supervisor, have you reviewed Human Resources' policies and procedures, including conduct and disciplinary guidelines, performance appraisal systems, and interviewing guidelines?
- Have you discussed initial work assignments?
- Have you accompanied your new employees to meet with colleagues and team members and talk about their responsibilities and how they relate to the new staff members?
- Have you explained social matters, toured the office and building, and reviewed building security measures?
- Have you helped the new hire understand the corporate culture and history?

- "Did everything go well when filling out your new hire paperwork and when meeting your pre-hire appointments?"
- "How is orientation going?"
- "Do you have any questions about your orientation schedule?"
- "How did your first day go?"
- "Was someone always available to answer your questions whenever you had them?"
- "Did anything happen today that concerns you in any way?"
- "Did people meet with you on a timely basis, and were your meetings productive and informative?"
- "Have you been introduced to peers, supervisors, and others? Do you have a schedule in place for this?"
- "What do you need at this point?"

First Week Checklist

- Have you conducted an interview with your new hire to further uncover strengths and areas in which the new employee has an interest in developing?

- Have you discussed with your new employee the process for monitoring and review what will take place during the initial months of her employment? Aside from day-to-day communications, your process should include regular meetings where discussions can take place on the previous week's performance, new assignments, and any issues. Give the employee the opportunity to ask questions.

- Have you outlined a complete review of the organization, including mission and values, structure, goals and objectives, strategies, introductions to other employees, supervisory meetings clarifying roles and responsibilities?

- If yours is a virtual environment, have you ensured that the new employee receives calls from other team members, and have you sent photos and bios of each of them?

- Have you provided your new employee with a list of go-to people or departments that can easily respond to normal inquiries such as technology, office supplies, or facilities matters?

- Have you successfully assigned "mentors" to help show your new employee the ropes? Are your mentors people who have been with the company for a longer length of time, so they can offer valuable social and cultural integration to enhance the understanding of the organization? Their roles should be to offer culture insights, explain the organizational structure, and help new employees understand why things happen the way they do. Mentors should exhibit the behavior and results-orientation that you want from all employees. The role can be as simple as going to lunch once a week. Mentors should be well networked within an organization.

- Have you developed realistic expectations of the job and the employee's career potential with the company, and have you set up an early constructive feedback system?
- Have you paved the way for your new employee to develop collaborative relationships with key stakeholders and gain a comprehensive understanding of other areas within the organization's point of view and goals?
- Have you and your new employee developed and signed off on a six-month agreement of objectives and expectations?
- Have you given your new employee an opportunity to ask questions and give feedback on any issues that have come up during the first week?
- Have you provided an understanding of strategic direction, values, culture, and organizational changes?
- Have you focused your new employee on high-impact objectives necessary for success?
- Have you alerted your new employee to any inherited adverse situations or liabilities that need to be addressed?
- Have you identified potential derailers, and are you supporting your new employee's success?
- Have you built a six-month road map identifying

opportunities to deliver early results and outline goals and ways to achieve them to increase your employee's ability to make a positive impact?

- Have you set up a schedule to hold regular meetings to discuss challenges, cultural fit, snags, and 30-/60-/90-day plans?
- Have you set up a lunch for your new employee with a new staff member each day?
- Are you providing new employees time each day to ask questions and identify areas of need?
- Have you identified players who have the greatest potential to block your new employee's success? If so, have you developed a relationship-building strategy that includes an in-person introduction with you?

After week one, be sure to ask your new employee these questions:

- "Is there any aspect of your job that you wished we would have focused more attention on during your first week?"
- "Is there anything you would suggest we change to help other new employees get acclimated during their first week on the job?"
- "What was the best part of your first week?"
- "What were some of the challenges you dealt with during this week?"
- "How well do you think you are doing so far on the job?"
- "Was someone always available to answer any questions you had?"
- "Have you been introduced to everyone?"
- "Do you feel that everyone is welcoming to new employees?"
- "Is there something that comes to mind that hasn't been explained to you well?"

Checklist for One Month and Beyond

- Have you mapped out your new employee's network and made introductions? An employee's effectiveness generally derives from a person's web of relationships. Introduce your employee to people she needs to know in order to carry out job responsibilities, from whom she will need information, to whom she will provide information, and to people who are resourceful, who know how to get things done and move projects to completion. Include people who can provide experiences and knowledge surrounding company values.

- Have you assigned your new employee to short educational stints, for example, with customers, customer service, and salespeople to understand the customer experience? Introductions to employees with longer tenure can also provide tremendous value, so include a cross section.

- When setting up meetings for your employee, have you explained what he needs to learn from each person? Follow up and reinforce the importance of these relationships by asking "To whom have you spoken, what have you learned, and how do you see yourself helping them?" Document this information in monthly status reports.

- Have you invited your new employee to meetings outside his work responsibility to gain valuable insights and perspectives into other areas of the company?

- New employees come with new perspectives and ideas, so encourage them to share new ideas and approaches.

Have you scheduled meetings where new employees can share ideas?

- Have you conducted peer reviews and 360-degree performance reviews? Ask people who work with the new hire after 60 days to eliminate bias that only one person may have.
- Have you created a strategic plan that identifies accountabilities and responsibilities, performance standards, and a personal development plan?
- Have you conducted meetings with key stakeholders to identify key issues the new employee can have an impact on?
- Every three months, have you surveyed the new employee to assess the effectiveness of on-boarding processes and to identify any ongoing issues?
- Have you celebrated completion of the first month and recognized all mentors?
- Have you developed goals and expectations collaboratively with the new employee, as well as a formal and informal training plan?
- Have you developed an agreement on communication and performance feedback needs and included time frames for formal and informal evaluations and follow up?
- Have you provided feedback on the new employee's quality of interaction with coworkers and supervisors?

After 30/60/90 days ask your new employee these questions:

- "What part of your job do you find most rewarding?"
- "What part of your job makes you feel most successful?"
- "Tell me about some of your successes during your [first/second/third] month."
- "Do you believe this job meets your expectations?"
- "Do you have any suggestions for improvements?"
- "Are there aspects of your job that you feel you need more training in?"
- "What areas of your job would you like more feedback on?"
- "Do you feel you are on track to meet your annual objectives?"
- "Explain how you are going to achieve your annual objectives or any barriers challenging your ability to meet objectives."

- "I would recommend ABC Company to my friends as a good place to work."
- "ABC Company's values are consistent with my personal values."
- "There are no barriers to my doing a good job."
- "The work that I am responsible for makes a difference to this organization."
- "I am trusted to make meaningful decisions in my day-to-day activities."
- "I am paid fairly, given my responsibilities and performance."

Celebrate future milestones with new employees to cultivate pride in working for your organization, especially their first-year anniversary. Some ideas for recognition include:

- Send a personal note, thanking the employee for her first year of service.
- Get the employee's first-year perceptions.
- Review and develop future goals where appropriate.
- Share success stories with others about departments and people.

Remember to always demonstrate caring and appreciation for the new employee and the mentors who support the process.

About the Authors

Lori Davila is a nationally recognized executive coach and agent, who specializes in career and leadership development and in attracting exciting job leads for executive and outplacement clientele.

She writes a career and networking column for *The Atlanta Journal-Constitution* and regularly contributes to *The Wall Street Journal*. Lori's first book, *How to Choose the Right Person for the Right Job Every Time* (McGraw-Hill), includes 401 behavior-based and other interview questions for both hiring managers and job seekers. She has also contributed to several best-selling résumé books including *Resumes That Knock 'Em Dead*, and she is a contributing author to *Conscious Women Conscious Careers*. Lori has appeared on numerous radio programs and in international publications and newspapers. She can be reached at lori@ atlantacareermarketing.com.

Margot King is a 25-year human resources veteran and nationally recognized pioneer in the art of inter-viewing, selection, and hiring strategies. She is the Founder and CEO of OnSite Resource Solutions LLC, a company that specializes in talent acquisition and leadership development programs for corporations globally.

Ms. King has been the writer, producer, and host of the nationally syndicated radio talk show *Job Talk with Margot King*, with over 300 shows to her credit. She is an on-line blog contributor for *The Atlanta Journal-Constitution*, and has been a columnist for *Atlanta Woman* magazine and for AJCJOBS.com. She is a sought-after speaker, regarding employment trends and empowerment of women executives. She can be reached at mking@onsite-rs.com.

PERFECT PHRASES
for...

MANAGERS

Perfect Phrases for Managers and Supervisors

Perfect Phrases for Setting Performance Goals

Perfect Phrases for Performance Reviews

Perfect Phrases for Motivating and Rewarding Employees

Perfect Phrases for Documenting Employee Performance Problems

Perfect Phrases for Business Proposals and Business Plans

Perfect Phrases for Customer Service

Perfect Phrases for Executive Presentations

Perfect Phrases for Business Letters

Perfect Phrases for the Sales Call

Perfect Phrases for Perfect Hiring

Perfect Phrases for Building Strong Teams

Perfect Phrases for Dealing with Difficult People

YOUR CAREER

Perfect Phrases for the Perfect Interview

Perfect Phrases for Resumes

Perfect Phrases for Negotiating Salary & Job Offers

Perfect Phrases for Cover Letters